THIS BOOK BELONGS TO :

_____

_____

Funny with

Coordinates

Graph Lines in Slope-Intercept Form

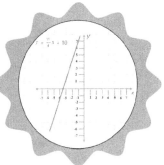

Grades 7-9

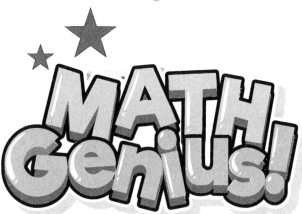

Table of Contents
Coordinates

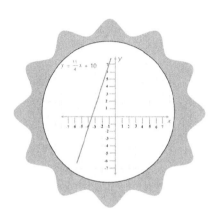

Grades 7-9

Graph Lines in Slope-Intercept Form

- Axis Points in Quadrant 7 ....(P.1 - 26)
- Axis Points in Quadrant 8 ....(P.27 - 52)
- Axis Points in Quadrant 9 ....(P.53 - 78)
- Axis Points in Quadrant 10 ....(P.79- 104)

Answer key... (P.105 - 140)

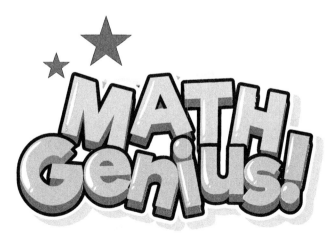

Name :   Date :

Timer :   Score :   / 100

Math Challenge

Slope-Intercept Form M1702-001

Draw the graph of each line.

1. $y = -x + 7$

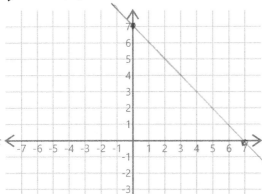

2. $y = \frac{3}{2}x - 2$

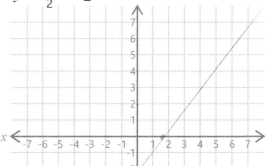

3. $y = \frac{1}{2}x + 6$

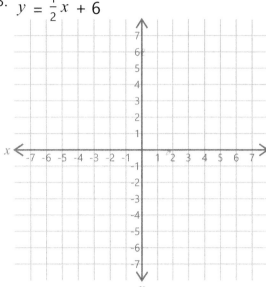

4. $y = \frac{9}{4}x + 6$

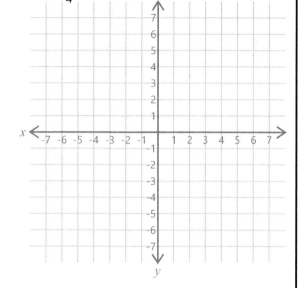

5. $y = -x + 5$

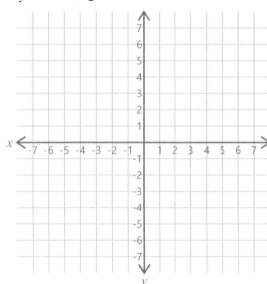

6. $y = x + 5$

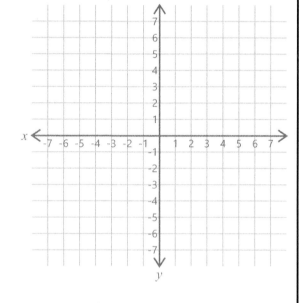

7. $y = \frac{-7}{4}x - 6$

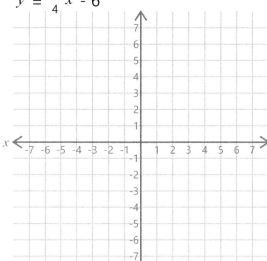

8. $y = \frac{1}{4}x$

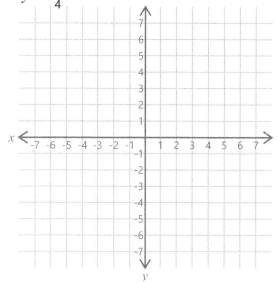

9. $y = \frac{1}{4}x + 3$

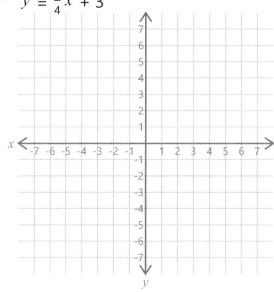

10. $y = \frac{1}{2}x - 7$

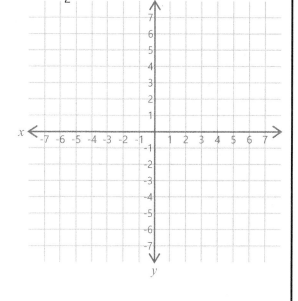

Slope-Intercept Form M1702-001

11. $y = 3x - 5$

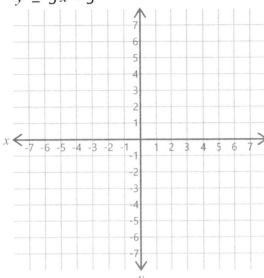

12. $y = \dfrac{-1}{4}x - 2$

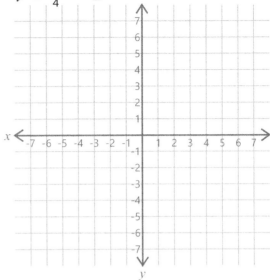

13. $y = \dfrac{-11}{4}x + 6$

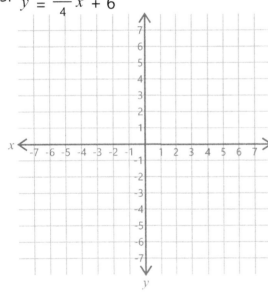

14. $y = \dfrac{-3}{2}x - 3$

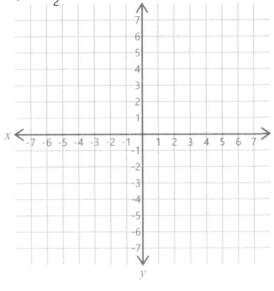

Slope-Intercept Form M1702-001

15. $y = \frac{3}{4}x - 1$

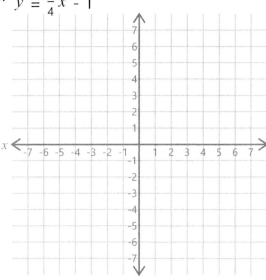

16. $y = \frac{-5}{4}x - 1$

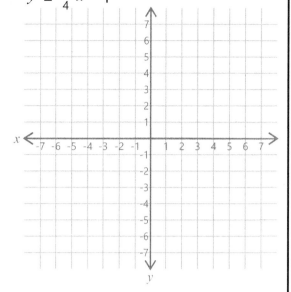

17. $y = x$

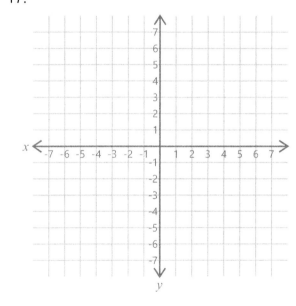

18. $y = \frac{-3}{2}x$

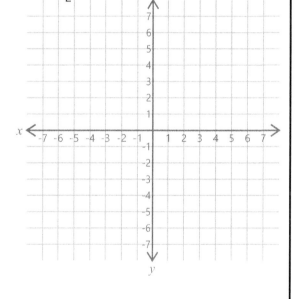

Slope-Intercept Form M1702-001

19. $y = -x + 6$

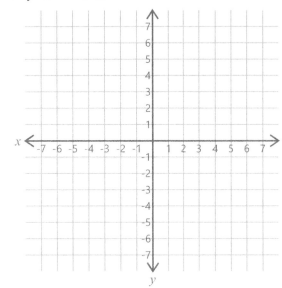

20. $y = \frac{1}{2}x + 3$

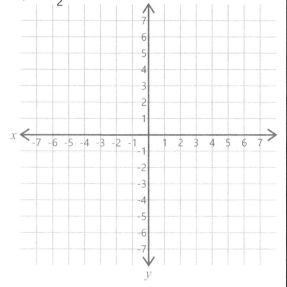

21. $y = \frac{-5}{2}x + 5$

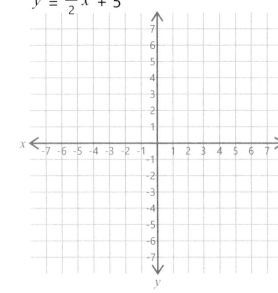

22. $y = 3x + 2$

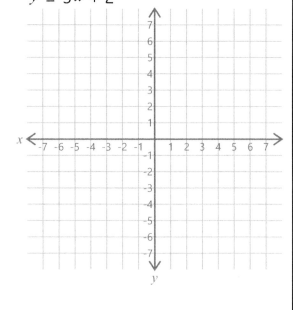

23. $y = \dfrac{-1}{2}x - 5$

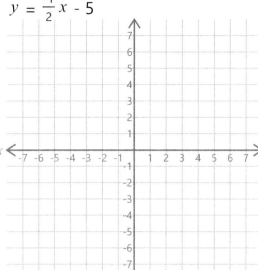

24. $y = x - 4$

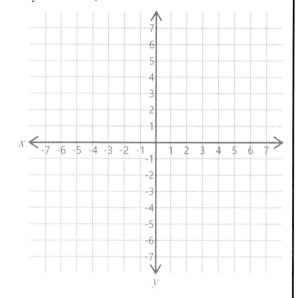

25. $y = -2x - 1$

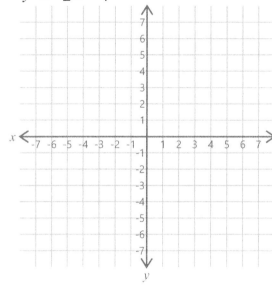

26. $y = \dfrac{-1}{2}x - 2$

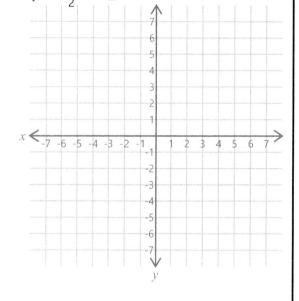

Slope-Intercept Form M1702-001

27. $y = \frac{9}{4}x - 3$

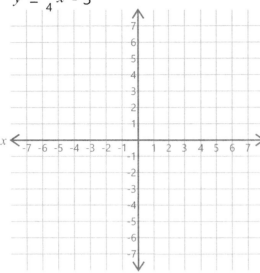

28. $y = \frac{-9}{4}x - 5$

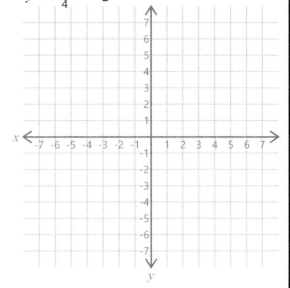

29. $y = \frac{1}{4}x - 2$

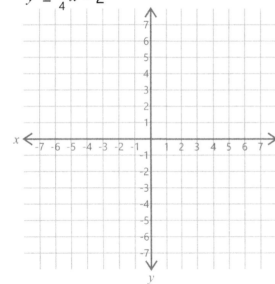

30. $y = \frac{-3}{4}x + 3$

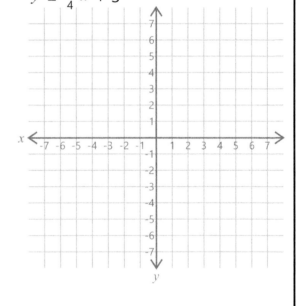

Slope-Intercept Form M1702-001

31. $y = \dfrac{-5}{4}x + 6$

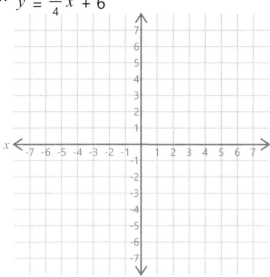

32. $y = \dfrac{1}{4}x - 4$

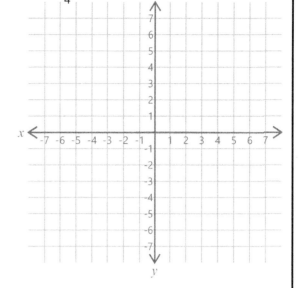

33. $y = -2x + 3$

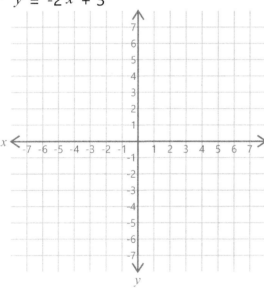

34. $y = \dfrac{5}{2}x + 7$

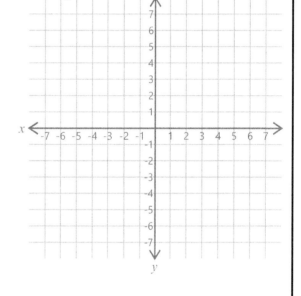

Slope-Intercept Form M1702-001

35. $y = -2x + 2$

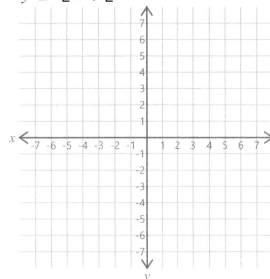

36. $y = -2x + 5$

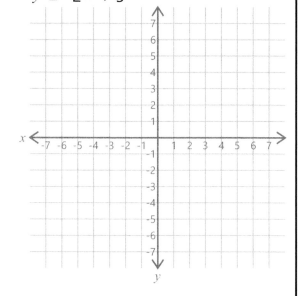

37. $y = \dfrac{11}{4}x - 6$

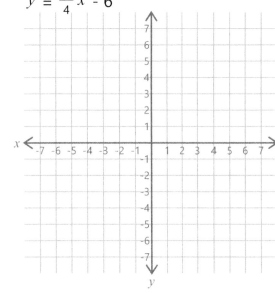

38. $y = -2x + 4$

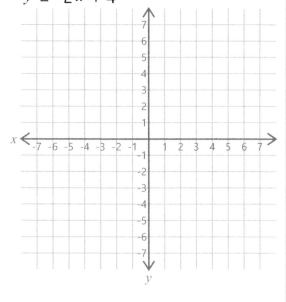

Slope-Intercept Form M1702-001

39. $y = 3x + 6$

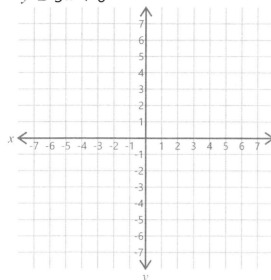

40. $y = \dfrac{-3}{2}x - 7$

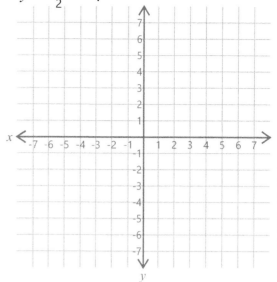

41. $y = x - 2$

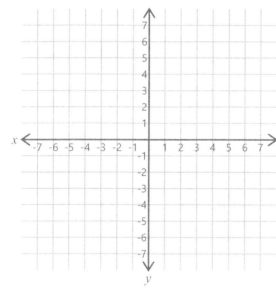

42. $y = \dfrac{-3}{4}x - 6$

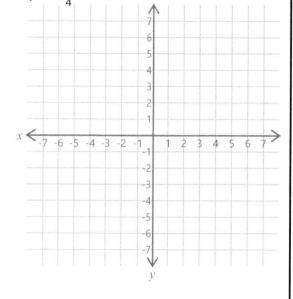

43. $y = -3x + 7$

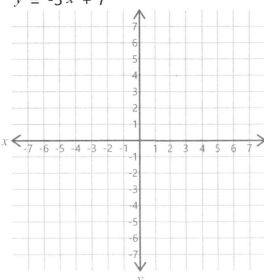

44. $y = \dfrac{-11}{4}x + 2$

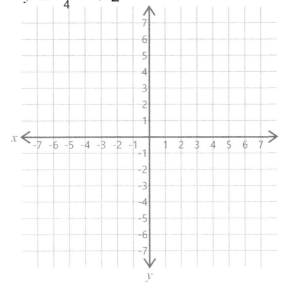

45. $y = \dfrac{-5}{2}x - 5$

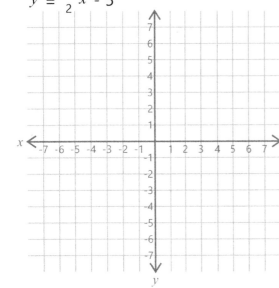

46. $x = 7$

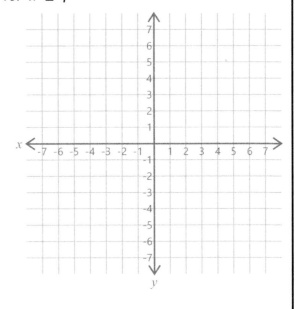

Slope-Intercept Form M1702-001

47. $y = \dfrac{-3}{4}x - 5$

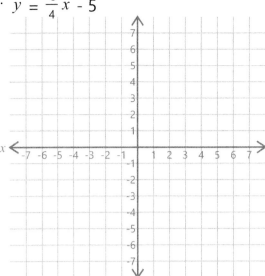

48. $y = \dfrac{-5}{4}x + 4$

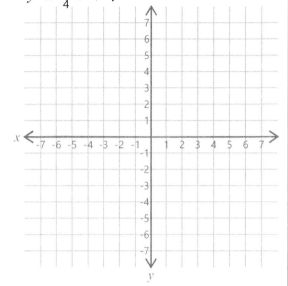

49. $y = \dfrac{-7}{4}x + 7$

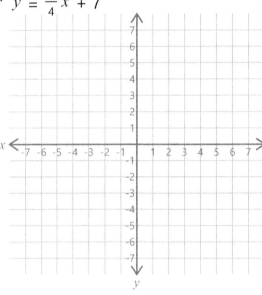

50. $y = \dfrac{-1}{2}x - 7$

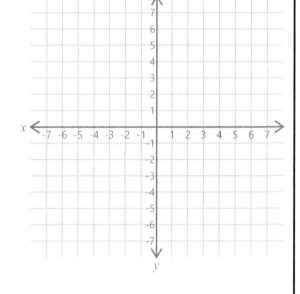

51. $x = 3$

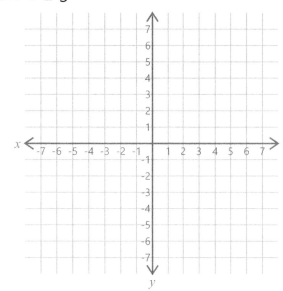

52. $y = \dfrac{-1}{4}x - 1$

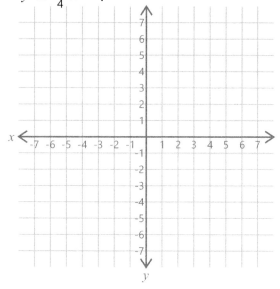

53. $y = \dfrac{-1}{4}x + 2$

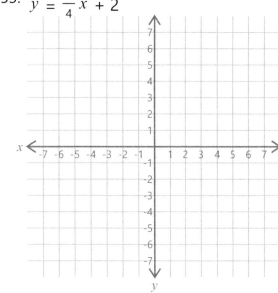

54. $y = \dfrac{9}{4}x + 2$

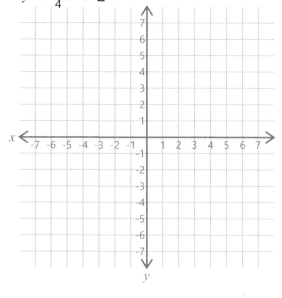

Slope-Intercept Form M1702-001

55. $y = \frac{3}{4}x + 5$

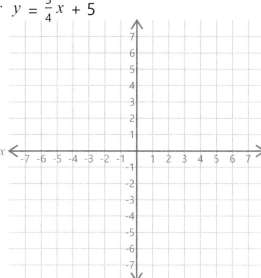

56. $x = -4$

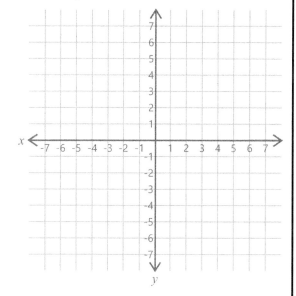

57. $y = \frac{-11}{4}x - 3$

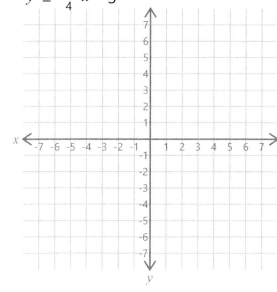

58. $y = \frac{1}{2}x - 6$

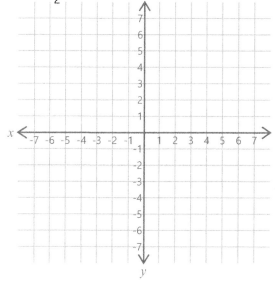

Slope-Intercept Form M1702-001

59. $y = \dfrac{5}{4}x + 4$

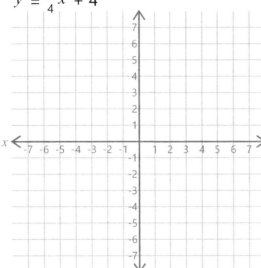

60. $y = 3x - 3$

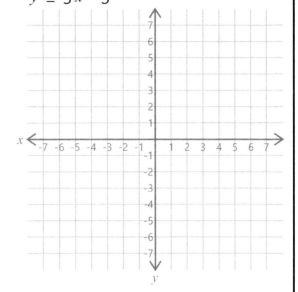

61. $y = x + 7$

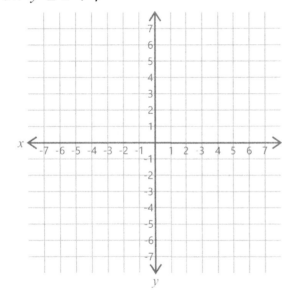

62. $y = \dfrac{11}{4}x - 4$

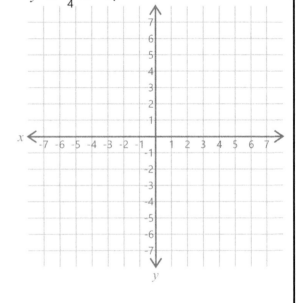

Slope-Intercept Form M1702-001

63. $y = \frac{3}{2}x + 2$

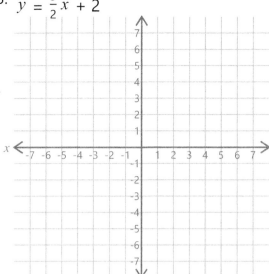

64. $y = 3x - 2$

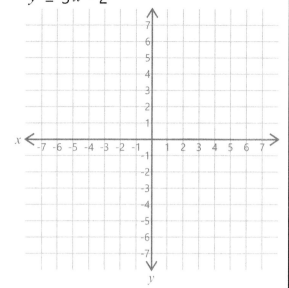

65. $y = \frac{-5}{2}x - 3$

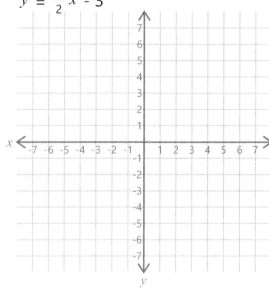

66. $y = -6$

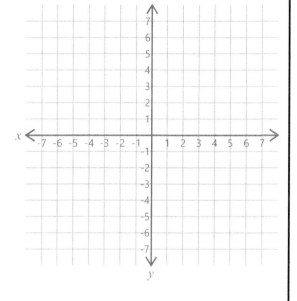

Slope-Intercept Form M1702-001

67. $y = \frac{-3}{2}x - 1$

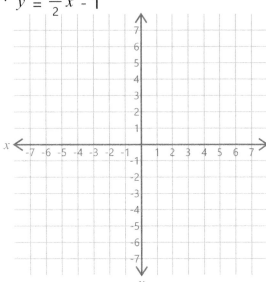

68. $y = \frac{-7}{4}x$

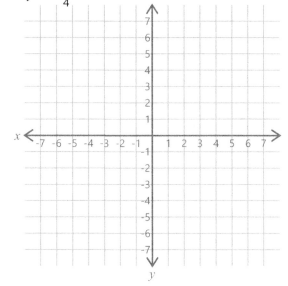

69. $y = \frac{3}{4}x - 5$

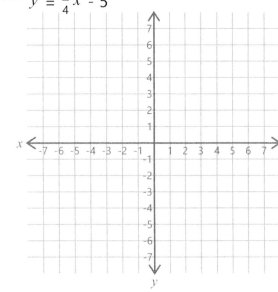

70. $y = x + 2$

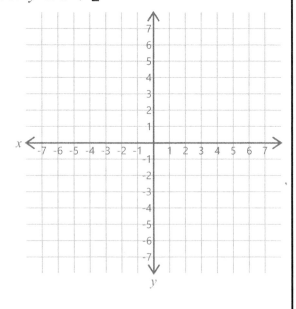

Slope-Intercept Form M1702-001

71. $y = -2x - 7$

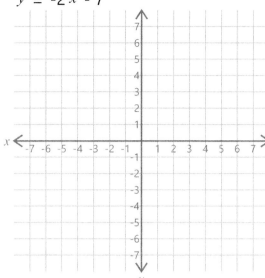

72. $y = \dfrac{7}{4}x + 6$

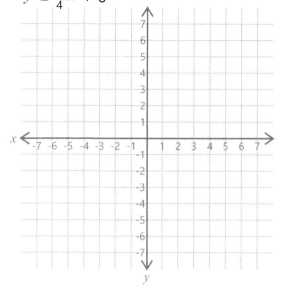

73. $y = \dfrac{-9}{4}x - 6$

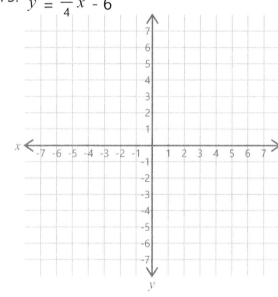

74. $y = \dfrac{-1}{4}x + 6$

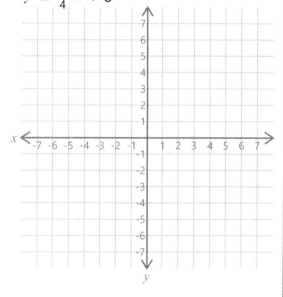

Slope-Intercept Form M1702-001

75. $y = \frac{-11}{4}x + 3$

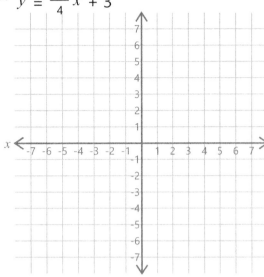

76. $y = \frac{1}{4}x - 6$

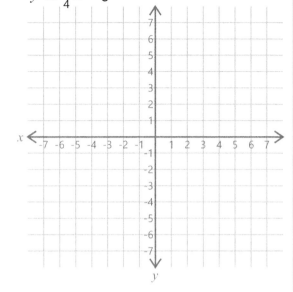

77. $y = \frac{-7}{4}x + 1$

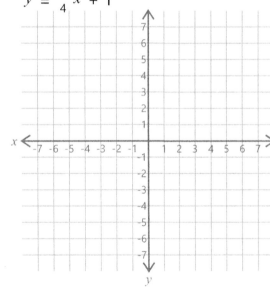

78. $y = \frac{11}{4}x + 6$

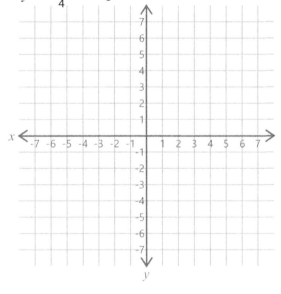

Slope-Intercept Form M1702-001

79. $y = \frac{3}{2}x + 3$

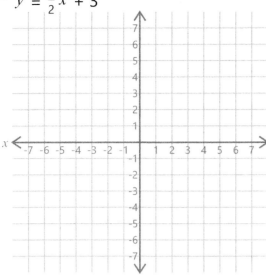

80. $y = \frac{3}{2}x + 7$

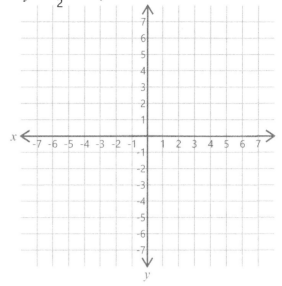

81. $y = \frac{5}{2}x - 2$

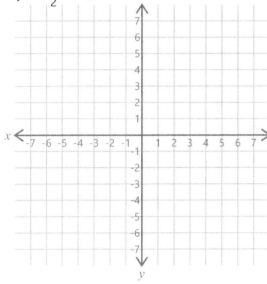

82. $y = \frac{-11}{4}x - 6$

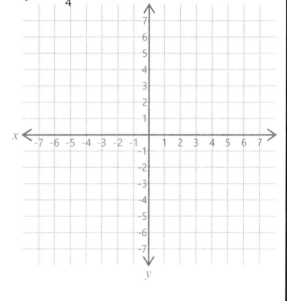

Slope-Intercept Form M1702-001

83. $y = \frac{11}{4}x - 5$

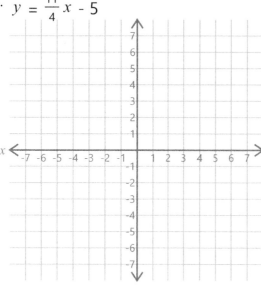

84. $y = \frac{-9}{4}x + 4$

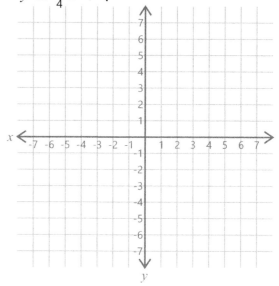

85. $y = \frac{3}{2}x - 7$

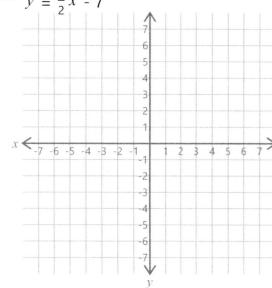

86. $y = \frac{9}{4}x + 5$

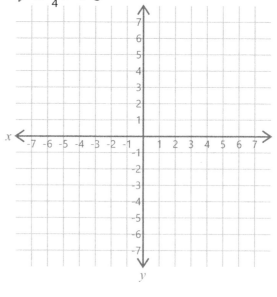

Slope-Intercept Form M1702-001

87. $y = \frac{1}{4}x + 5$

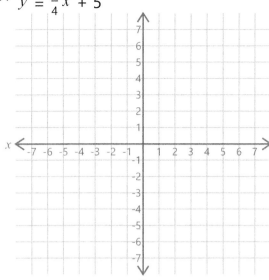

88. $y = \frac{-3}{2}x + 5$

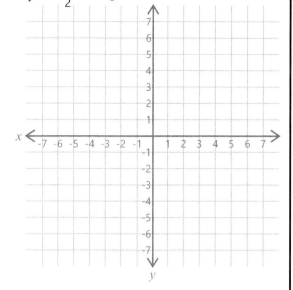

89. $y = \frac{3}{4}x - 2$

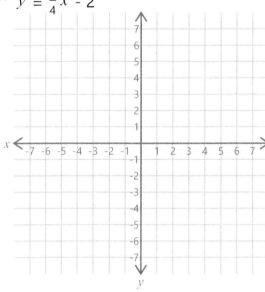

90. $y = \ + 6$

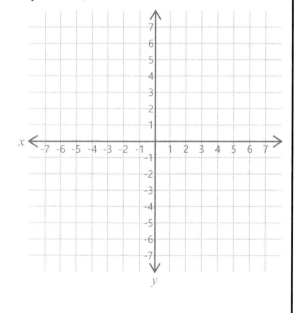

Slope-Intercept Form M1702-001

91. $y = \frac{-3}{2}x + 2$

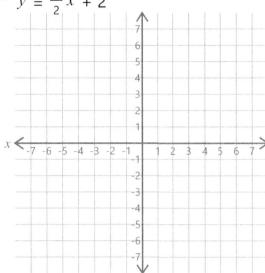

92. $y = \frac{3}{4}x + 3$

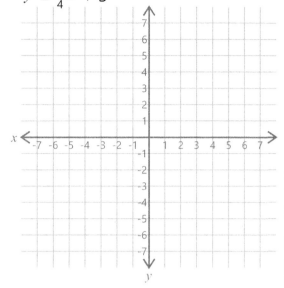

93. $y = \frac{-3}{2}x + 3$

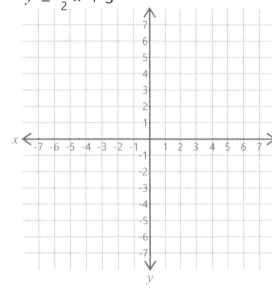

94. $y = \frac{11}{4}x - 1$

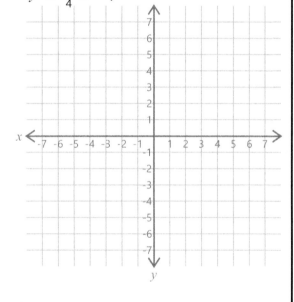

95. $y = -x + 4$

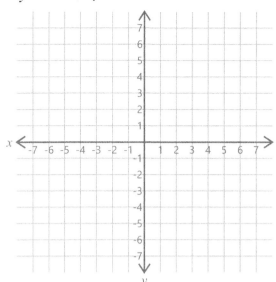

96. $y = \dfrac{-11}{4}x + 4$

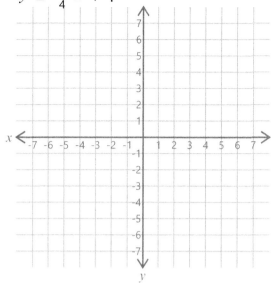

97. $y = -3x - 2$

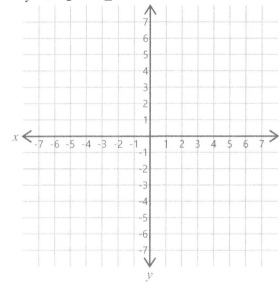

98. $x = 5$

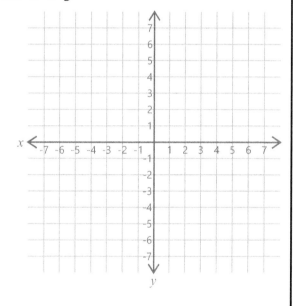

Slope-Intercept Form M1702-001

99. $y = \dfrac{-1}{2}x + 6$

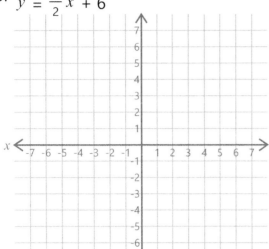

100. $y = \dfrac{1}{2}x - 2$

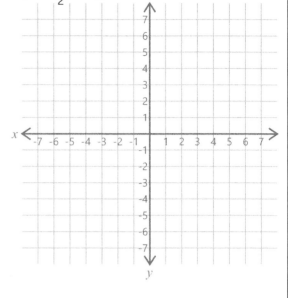

Slope-Intercept Form M1702-001

Name :

Date :

Timer :

Score : / 100

Math Challenge

Slope-Intercept Form M1702-002

Draw the graph of each line.

1. $y = \dfrac{3}{4}x - 5$

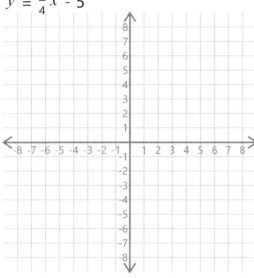

2. $y = -3x$

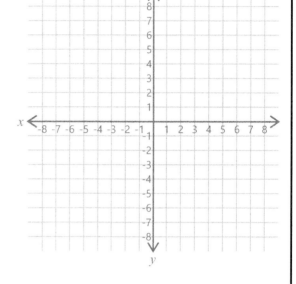

3. $y = \frac{-1}{2}x - 4$

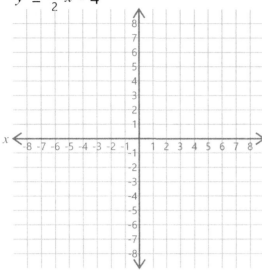

4. $y = \frac{-1}{2}x + 8$

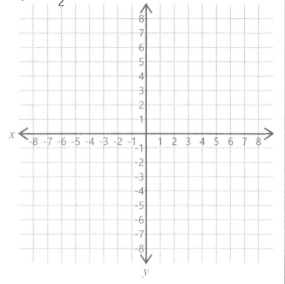

5. $y = -2x - 8$

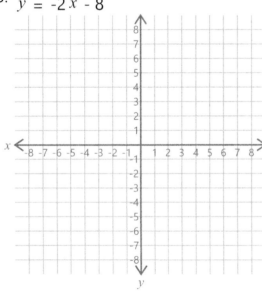

6. $y = \frac{5}{4}x + 2$

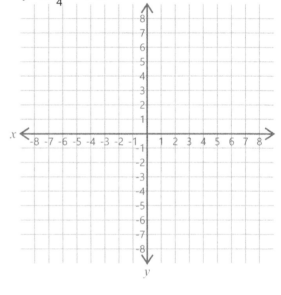

Slope-Intercept Form M1702-002

7. $y = \frac{-1}{2}x$

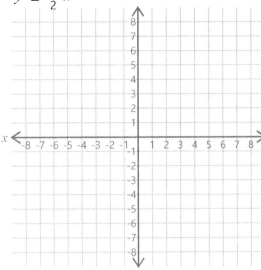

8. $y = \frac{7}{4}x + 7$

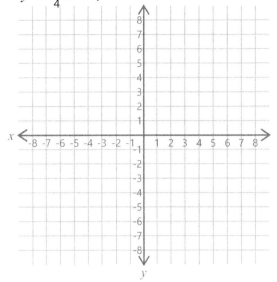

9. $x = 2$

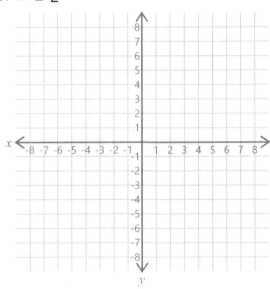

10. $y = \frac{-3}{4}x + 6$

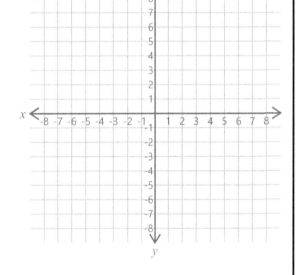

Slope-Intercept Form M1702-002

11. $y = 2x$

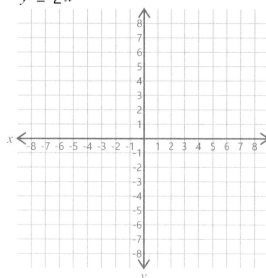

12. $y = \dfrac{-3}{4}x - 5$

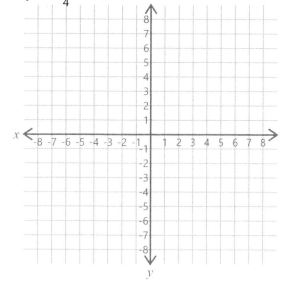

13. $y = \dfrac{-1}{4}x + 6$

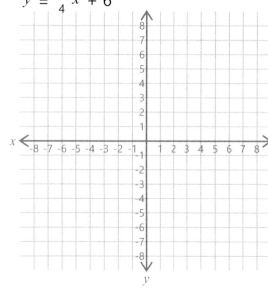

14. $y = \dfrac{-7}{4}x + 2$

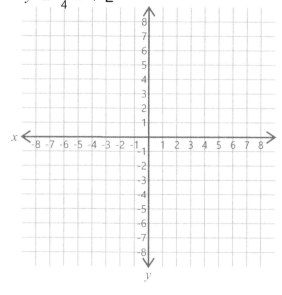

Slope-Intercept Form M1702-002

15. $y = \frac{-3}{2}x + 2$

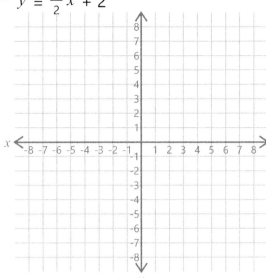

16. $y = \frac{7}{4}x - 2$

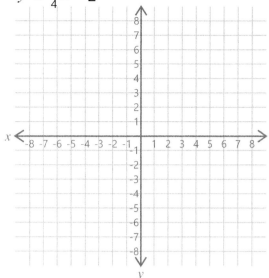

17. $y = \frac{5}{2}x - 1$

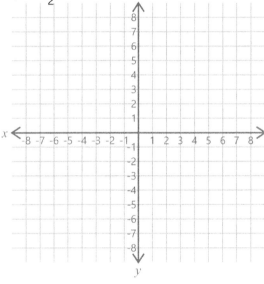

18. $y = \frac{5}{4}x - 2$

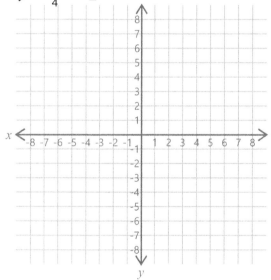

19. $y = \dfrac{7}{4}x$

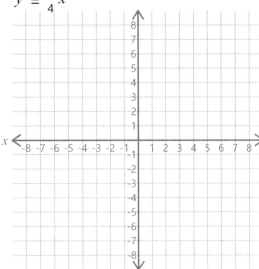

20. $y = -8$

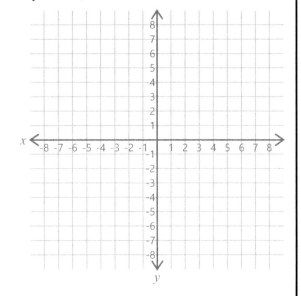

21. $y = \dfrac{-3}{2}x - 3$

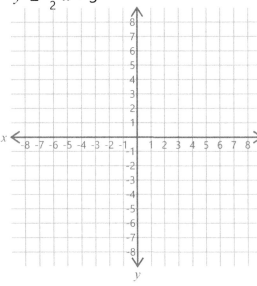

22. $y = \dfrac{1}{4}x - 3$

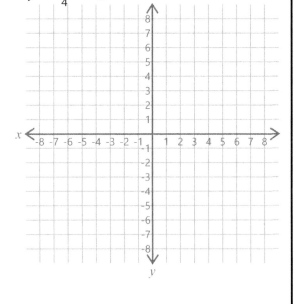

Slope-Intercept Form M1702-002

23. $y = -2x - 4$

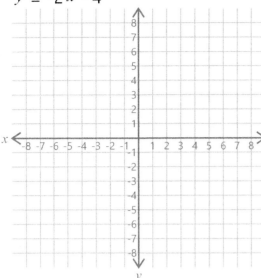

24. $y = \dfrac{-7}{4}x - 8$

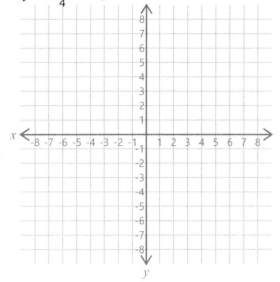

25. $y = \dfrac{11}{4}x - 5$

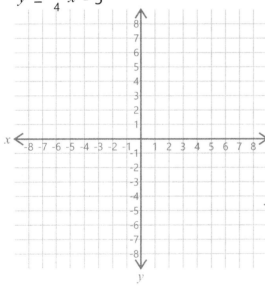

26. $y = \dfrac{3}{2}x - 5$

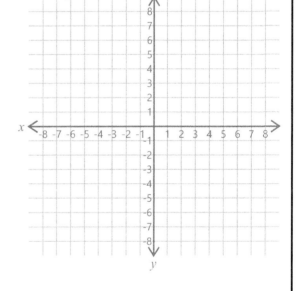

Slope-Intercept Form M1702-002

27. $y = -x + 4$

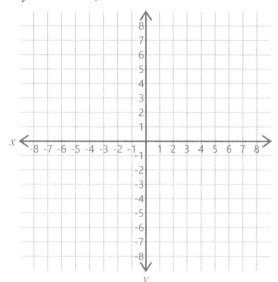

28. $y = \dfrac{-3}{4}x - 6$

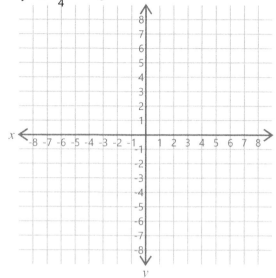

29. $y = \dfrac{9}{4}x + 5$

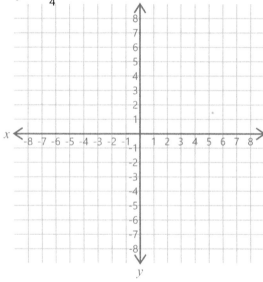

30. $y = \dfrac{-11}{4}x + 1$

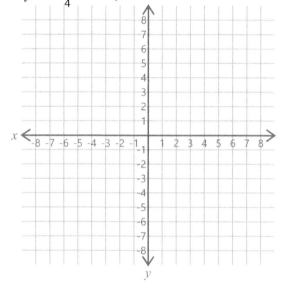

Slope-Intercept Form M1702-002

31. $y = \frac{-11}{4}x + 5$

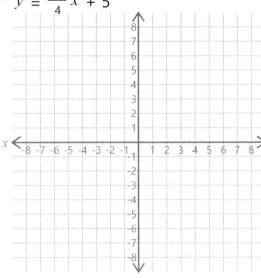

32. $y = \frac{3}{2}x + 2$

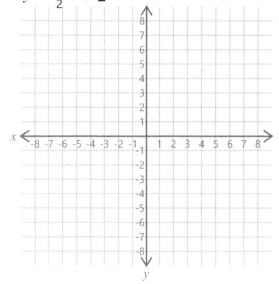

33. $y = 2x + 8$

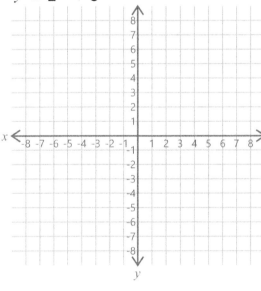

34. $y = \frac{9}{4}x - 2$

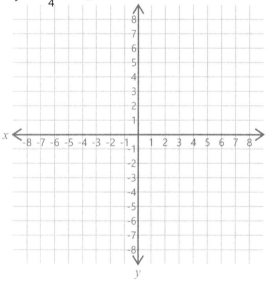

Slope-Intercept Form M1702-002

35. $y = -2x$

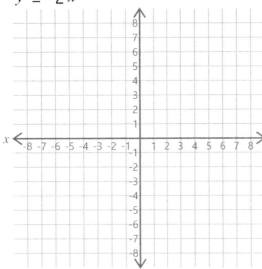

36. $y = -2x - 3$

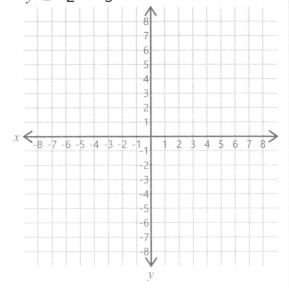

37. $y = \frac{3}{4}x$

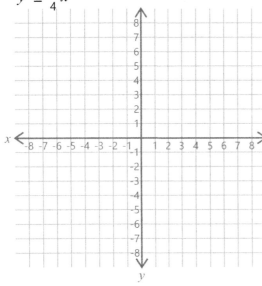

38. $x = -7$

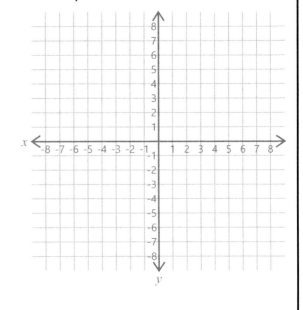

39. $y = -3x - 5$
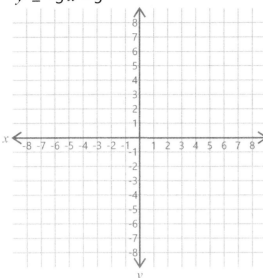

40. $y = x - 5$
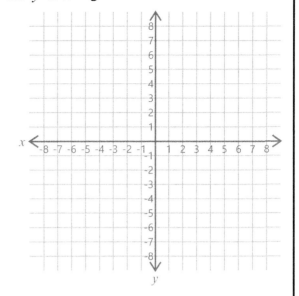

41. $y = \frac{7}{4}x - 8$
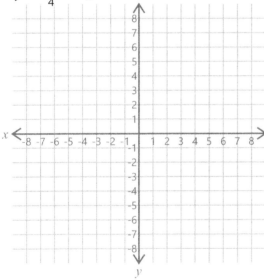

42. $y = \frac{5}{2}x + 1$
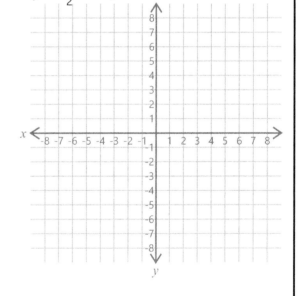

43. $y = \frac{-11}{4}x - 6$

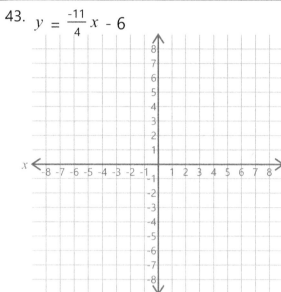

44. $y = \frac{-5}{2}x + 1$

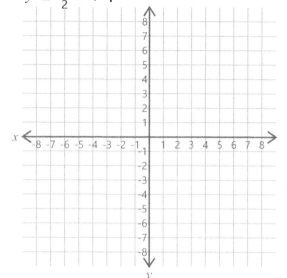

45. $y = \frac{1}{4}x + 7$

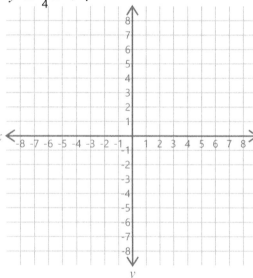

46. $y = \frac{-1}{2}x + 7$

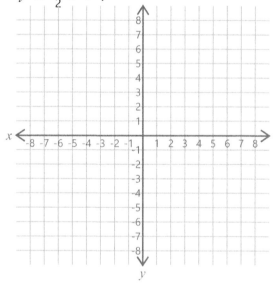

Slope-Intercept Form M1702-002

47. $x = 0$

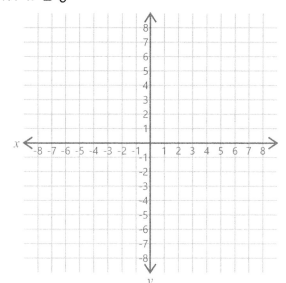

48. $y = \frac{3}{4}x + 7$

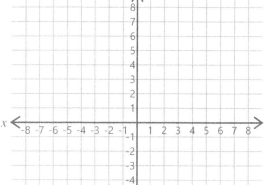

49. $y = \frac{-11}{4}x + 6$

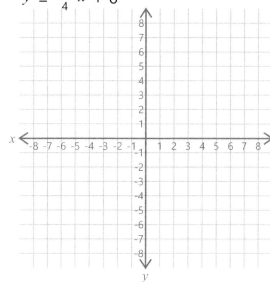

50. $y = \frac{-1}{4}x - 4$

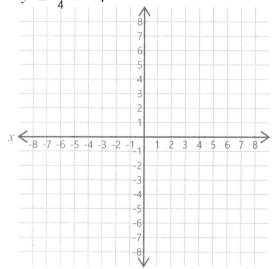

51. $y = \dfrac{-11}{4}x - 5$

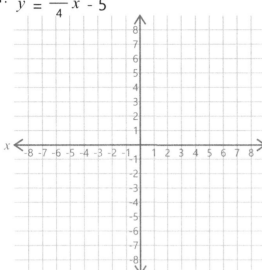

52. $y = \dfrac{-11}{4}x + 8$

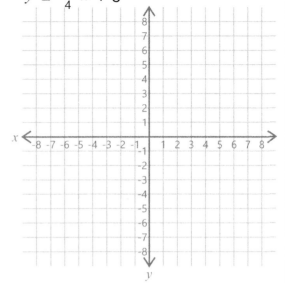

53. $y = \dfrac{-9}{4}x + 6$

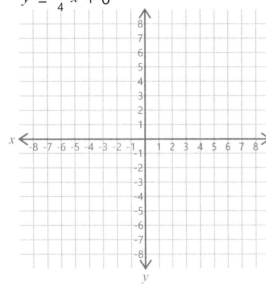

54. $y = \dfrac{-9}{4}x + 5$

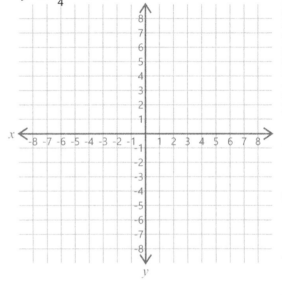

55. $y = 2x + 6$

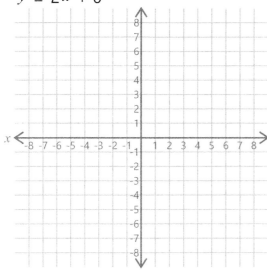

56. $y = 3x + 6$

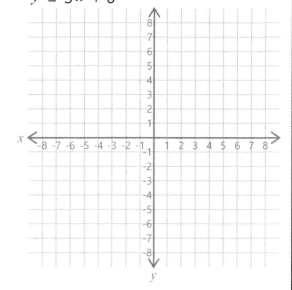

57. $y = -3x + 3$

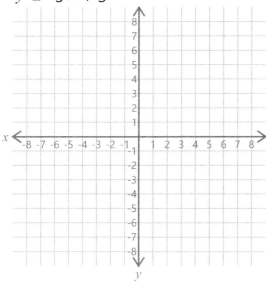

58. $y = \frac{3}{2}x + 3$

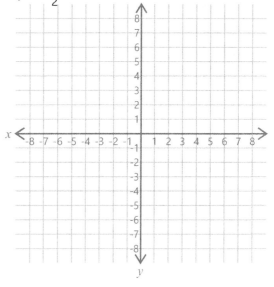

Slope-Intercept Form M1702-002

59. $y = \dfrac{-3}{2}x + 3$

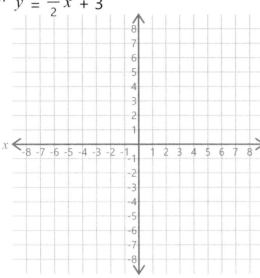

60. $y = \dfrac{5}{2}x - 4$

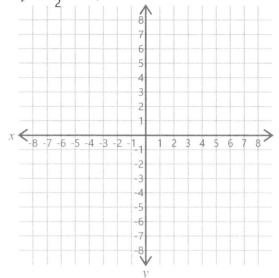

61. $y = \dfrac{5}{2}x - 5$

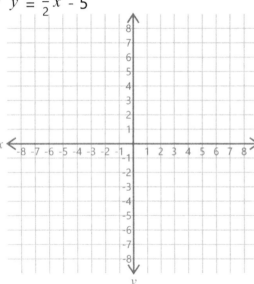

62. $y = \dfrac{-11}{4}x - 4$

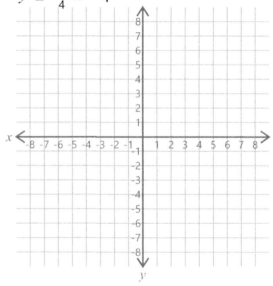

Slope-Intercept Form M1702-002

63. $y = -x - 7$

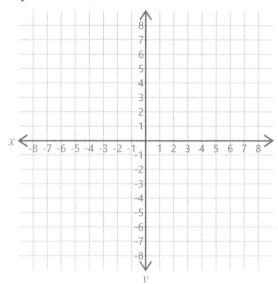

64. $y = \dfrac{11}{4}x - 8$

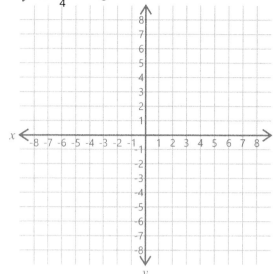

65. $y = -3x - 6$

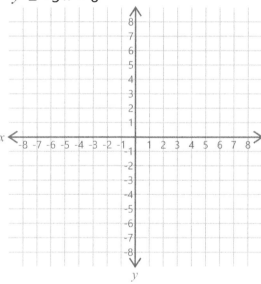

66. $x = 3$

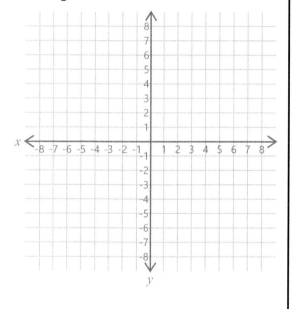

Slope-Intercept Form M1702-002

67. $y = -7$

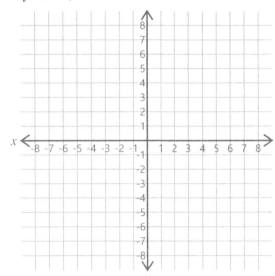

68. $y = \dfrac{-1}{2}x + 4$

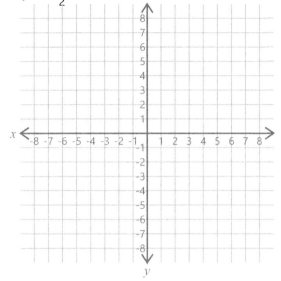

69. $y = \dfrac{-9}{4}x + 1$

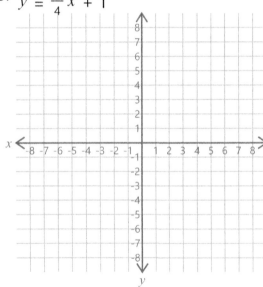

70. $x = -6$

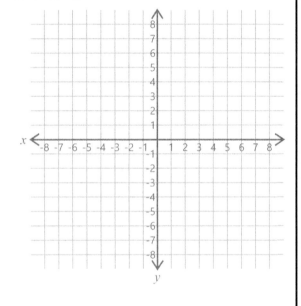

71. $y = \frac{-1}{4}x + 7$

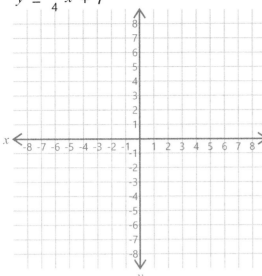

72. $y = \frac{-7}{4}x - 2$

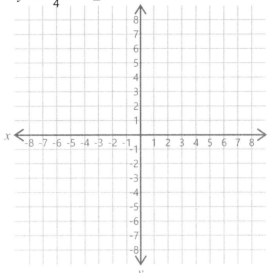

73. $y = x + 5$

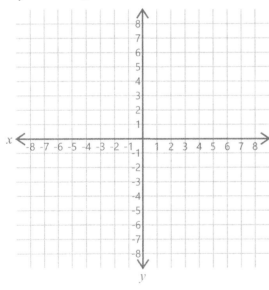

74. $y = x + 6$

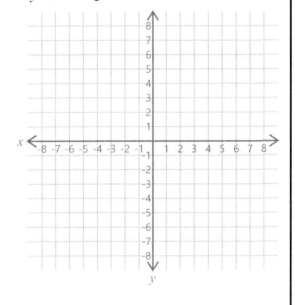

Slope-Intercept Form M1702-002

75. $y = -2x + 5$

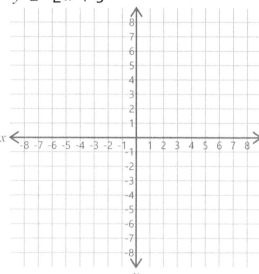

76. $y = \dfrac{5}{4}x - 8$

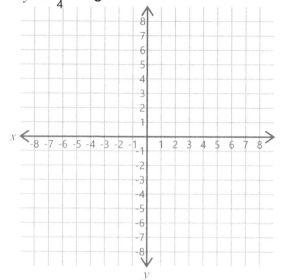

77. $y = 2x + 2$

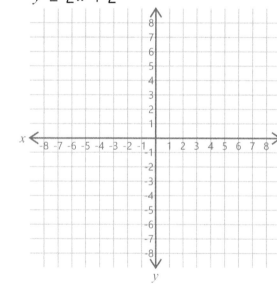

78. $y = 2x + 5$

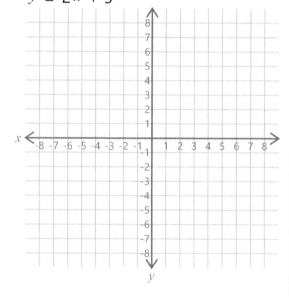

79. $y = \frac{3}{2}x - 7$

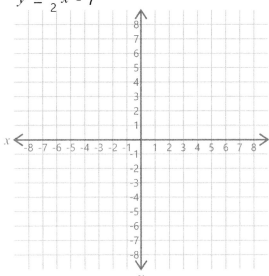

80. $y = \frac{-7}{4}x - 6$

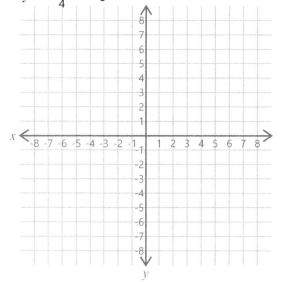

81. $y = x + 3$

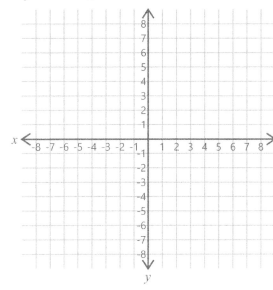

82. $y = \frac{5}{2}x - 6$

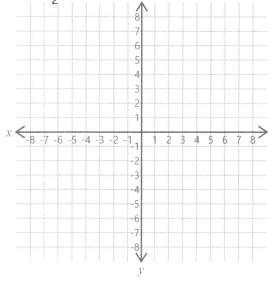

Slope-Intercept Form M1702-002

83. $y = \frac{-5}{2}x$

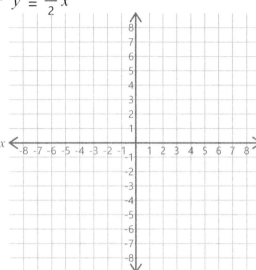

84. $y = \frac{-5}{4}x - 5$

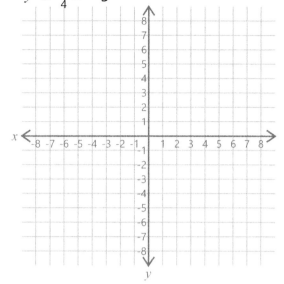

85. $y = x + 8$

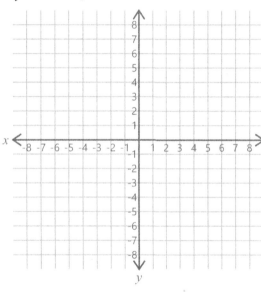

86. $y = \frac{9}{4}x + 3$

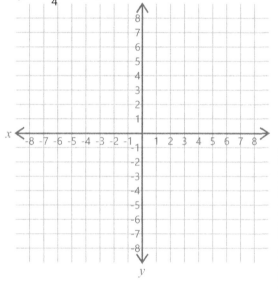

Slope-Intercept Form M1702-002

87. $y = \frac{1}{4}x + 8$

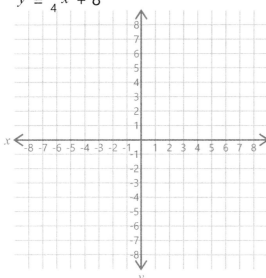

88. $y = \frac{3}{4}x - 6$

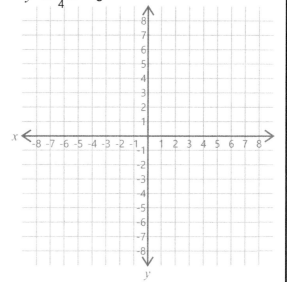

89. $y = + 3$

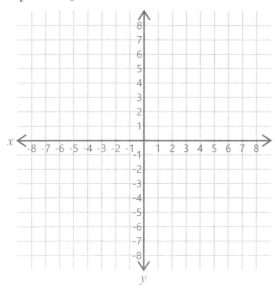

90. $y = \frac{-7}{4}x - 3$

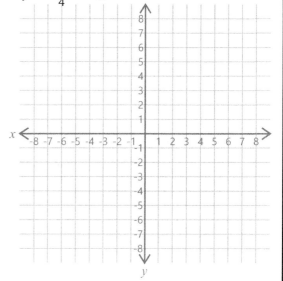

Slope-Intercept Form M1702-002

91. $y = \dfrac{-1}{4}x - 1$

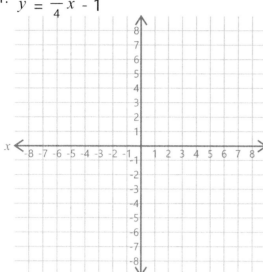

92. $y = \dfrac{-3}{4}x + 2$

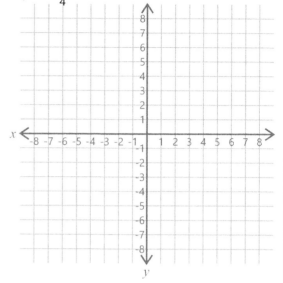

93. $y = -2x - 6$

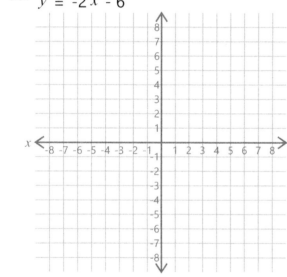

94. $y = \dfrac{-9}{4}x - 1$

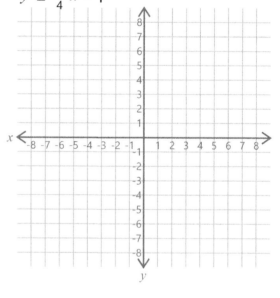

95. $y = \dfrac{-9}{4}x + 4$

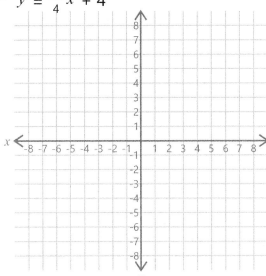

96. $y = \dfrac{-11}{4}x$

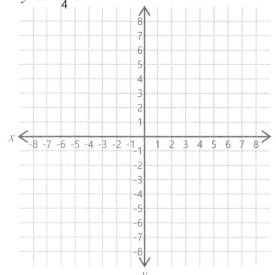

97. $y = \dfrac{7}{4}x + 2$

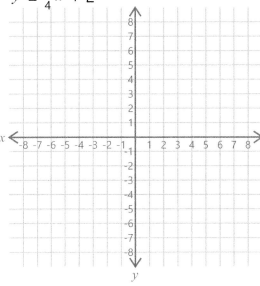

98. $y = \dfrac{1}{2}x$

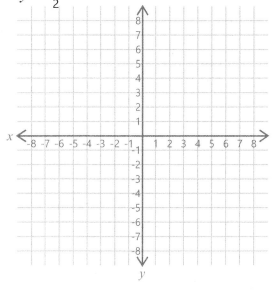

Slope-Intercept Form M1702-002

99. $y = \dfrac{-1}{2}x - 8$

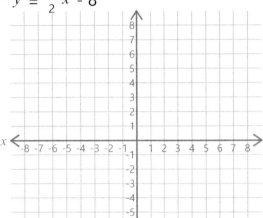

100. $y = \dfrac{-5}{4}x - 6$

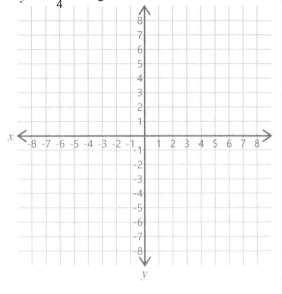

Slope-Intercept Form M1702-002

Name :

Date :

Timer :

Score : / 100

Math Challenge

Slope-Intercept Form M1702-003

Draw the graph of each line.

1. $y = \frac{-3}{2}x + 1$

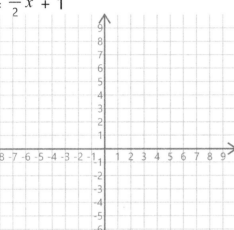

2. $y = \frac{-3}{4}x - 4$

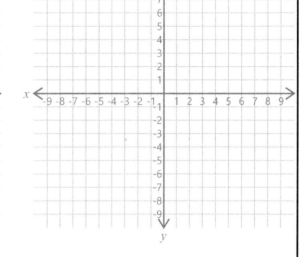

3. $y = -3x + 4$

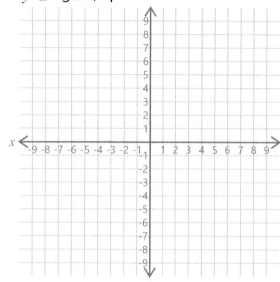

4. $y = \dfrac{-1}{4}x + 5$

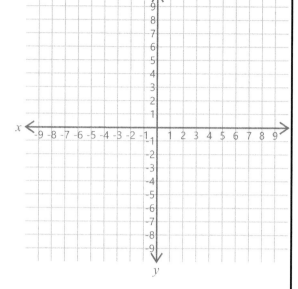

5. $y = \dfrac{5}{2}x - 8$

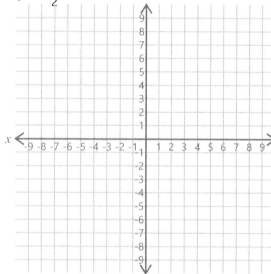

6. $y = \dfrac{-5}{4}x + 6$

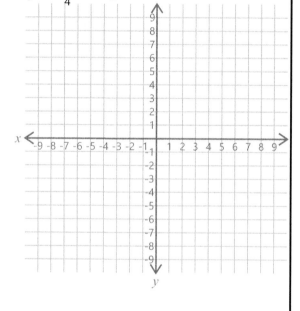

Slope-Intercept Form M1702-003

7. $y = -x + 2$

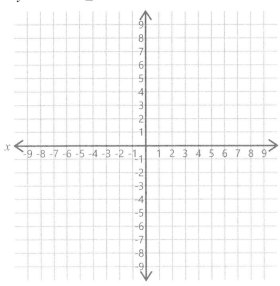

8. $y = \dfrac{9}{4}x + 9$

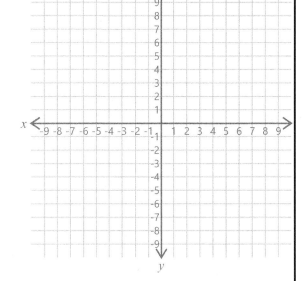

9. $y = \dfrac{3}{2}x - 4$

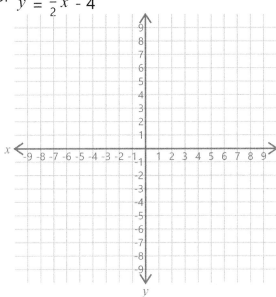

10. $y = \dfrac{3}{4}x - 9$

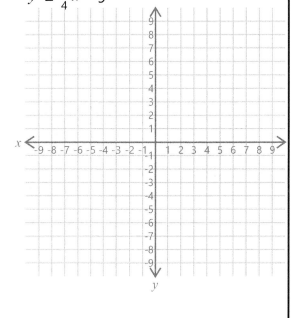

Slope-Intercept Form M1702-003

11. $y = \dfrac{-5}{4}x + 3$

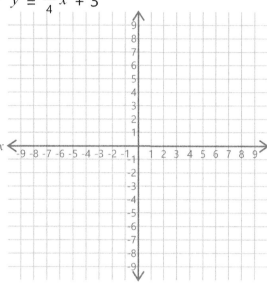

12. $y = \dfrac{9}{4}x - 4$

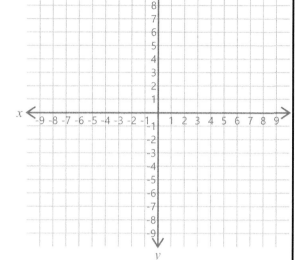

13. $y = \dfrac{-3}{2}x - 9$

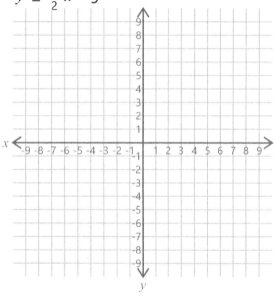

14. $y = \dfrac{-5}{4}x - 6$

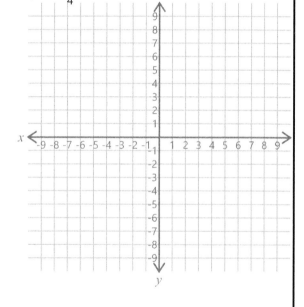

Slope-Intercept Form M1702-003

15. $y = -3x + 9$

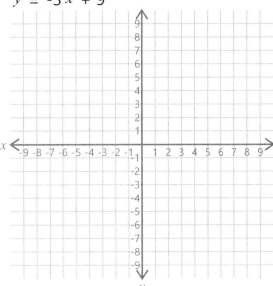

16. $y = \dfrac{-5}{2}x - 5$

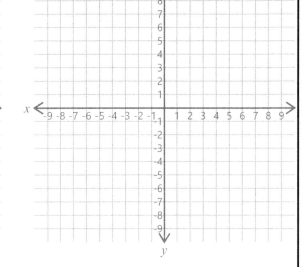

17. $y = \dfrac{1}{2}x + 6$

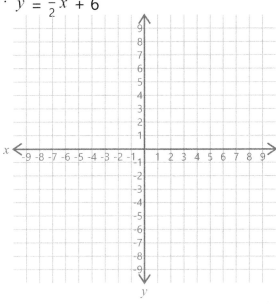

18. $y = \dfrac{-5}{2}x + 3$

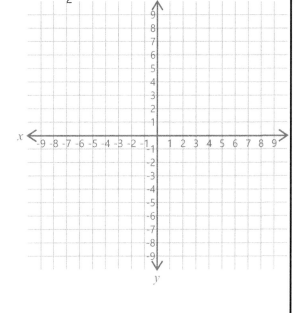

Slope-Intercept Form M1702-003

19. $y = +8$

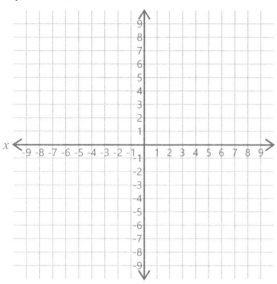

20. $y = 3x + 1$

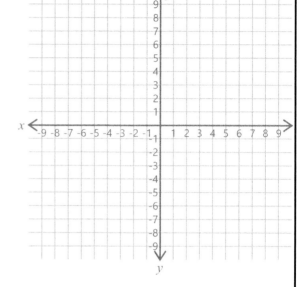

21. $y = \frac{5}{2}x - 2$

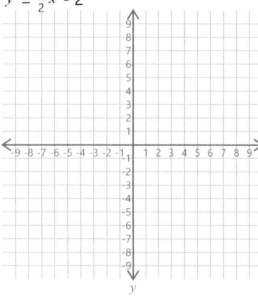

22. $y = \frac{-1}{4}x$

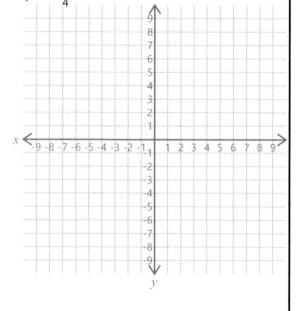

Slope-Intercept Form M1702-003

23. $y = \frac{5}{2}x + 7$

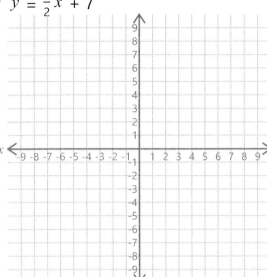

24. $y = -2x - 9$

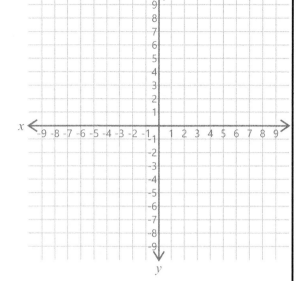

25. $y = x + 3$

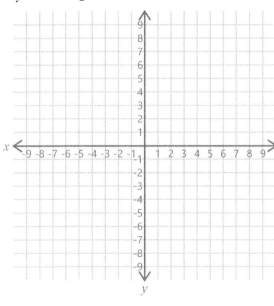

26. $y = \frac{7}{4}x + 6$

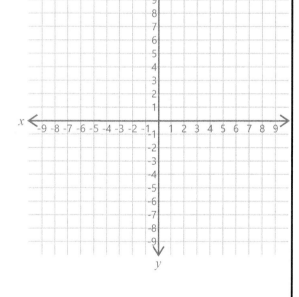

Slope-Intercept Form M1702-003

27. $y = \frac{1}{2}x + 4$

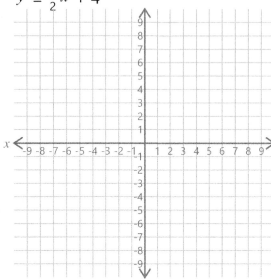

28. $y = \frac{1}{2}x + 3$

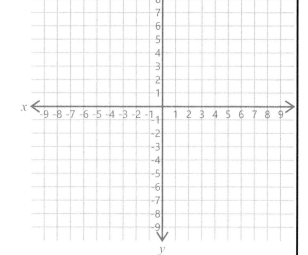

29. $y = \frac{3}{2}x - 8$

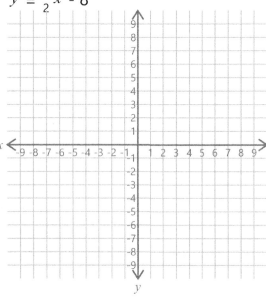

30. $y = \frac{-11}{4}x - 9$

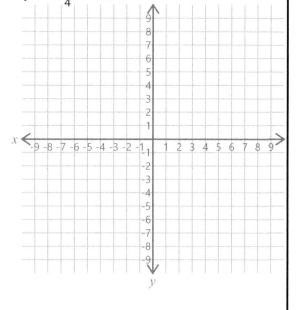

Slope-Intercept Form M1702-003

31. $y = \frac{-1}{2}x - 4$

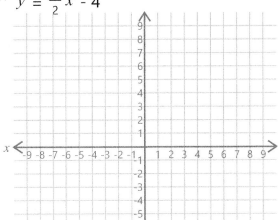

32. $y = \frac{7}{4}x + 7$

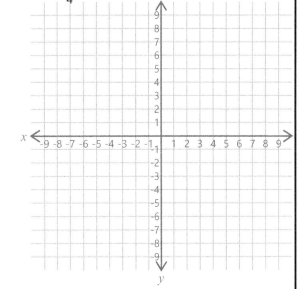

33. $x = -9$

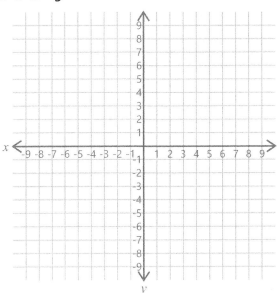

34. $y = \frac{-3}{2}x$

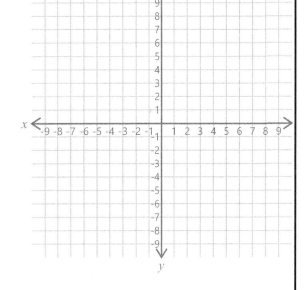

35. $y = \frac{1}{4}x - 6$

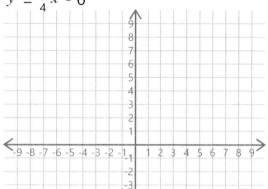

36. $y = +6$

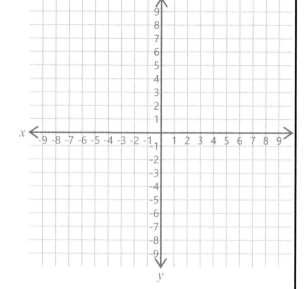

37. $y = \frac{-5}{4}x - 8$

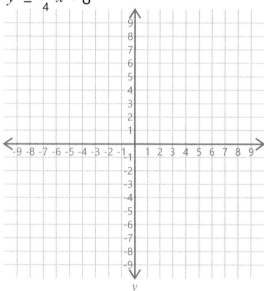

38. $y = \frac{-9}{4}x + 8$

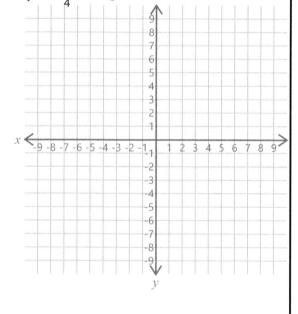

39. $y = \dfrac{-7}{4}x - 4$

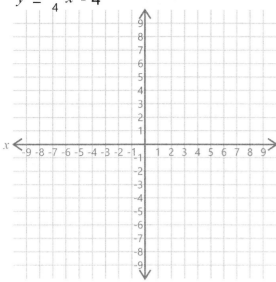

40. $y = \dfrac{-1}{4}x - 3$

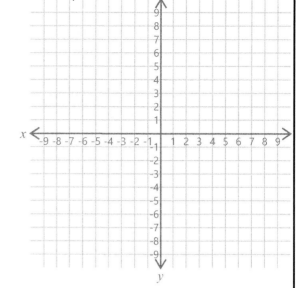

41. $y = \dfrac{5}{2}x - 5$

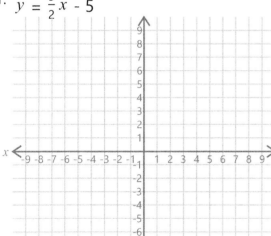

42. $y = \dfrac{1}{4}x - 3$

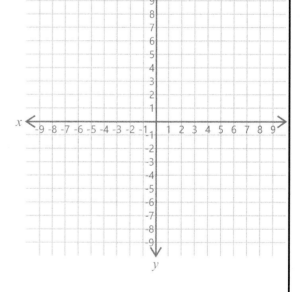

Slope-Intercept Form M1702-003

43. $y = x + 6$

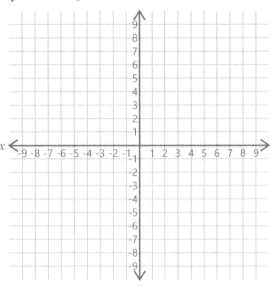

44. $y = \dfrac{-3}{2}x - 1$

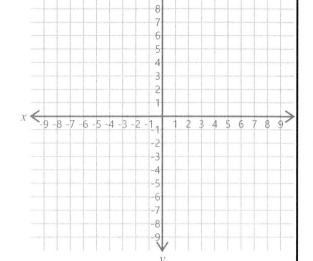

45. $y = \dfrac{11}{4}x - 2$

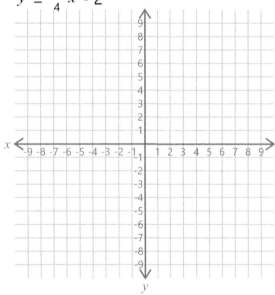

46. $y = \dfrac{-9}{4}x + 2$

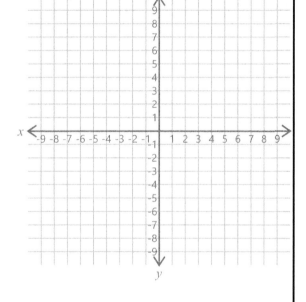

Slope-Intercept Form M1702-003

47. $y = x + 1$

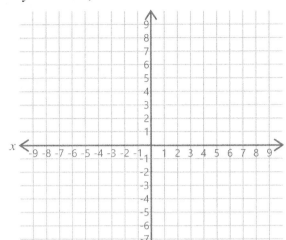

48. $y = \frac{1}{4}x - 1$

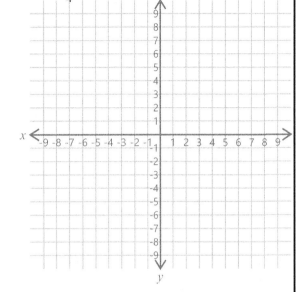

49. $y = -2x + 9$

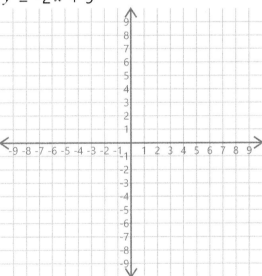

50. $y = \frac{1}{4}x$

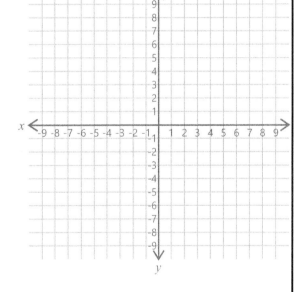

Slope-Intercept Form M1702-003

51. $y = \dfrac{-1}{4}x - 1$
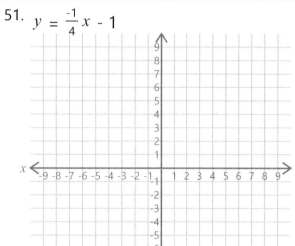

52. $y = x + 4$
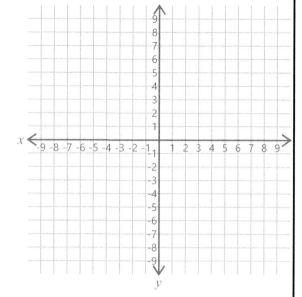

53. $y = \dfrac{-9}{4}x - 6$
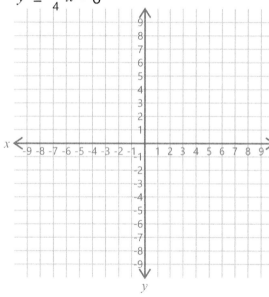

54. $y = \dfrac{7}{4}x - 1$
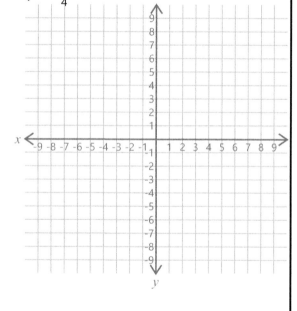

Slope-Intercept Form M1702-003

55. $y = \frac{-1}{2}x - 1$

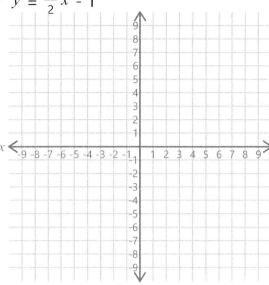

56. $y = \frac{-3}{2}x - 8$

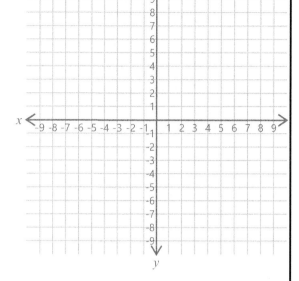

57. $y = \frac{-5}{4}x - 7$

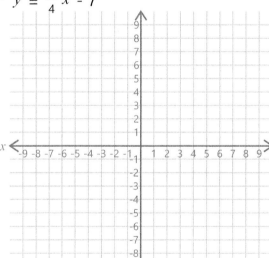

58. $y = 3x - 3$

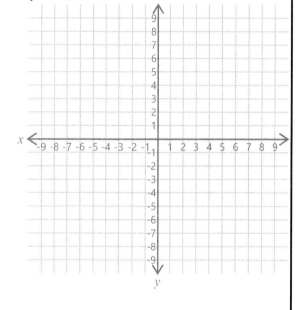

Slope-Intercept Form M1702-003

59. $y = \frac{7}{4}x + 3$

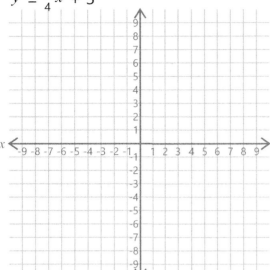

60. $y = \frac{7}{4}x - 6$

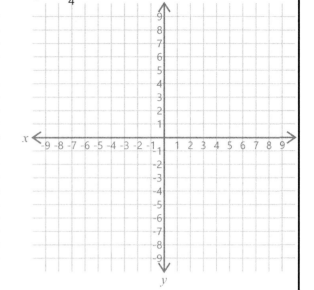

61. $y = \frac{7}{4}x - 8$

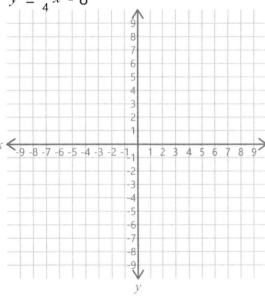

62. $y = -2x - 5$

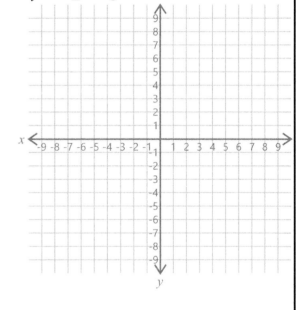

Slope-Intercept Form M1702-003

63. $y = \dfrac{7}{4}x - 7$

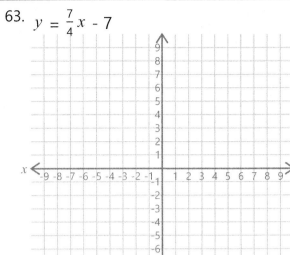

64. $y = -3x$

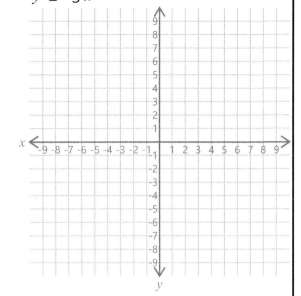

65. $y = 2x + 9$

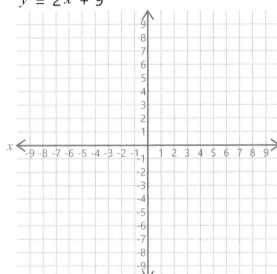

66. $y = \dfrac{9}{4}x - 6$

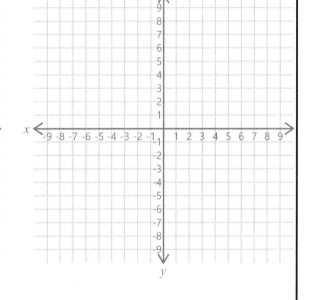

67. $y = 3x + 7$

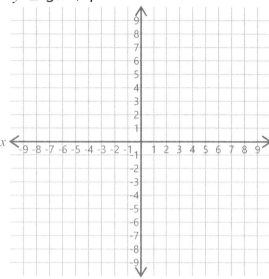

68. $y = \dfrac{-1}{2}x - 6$

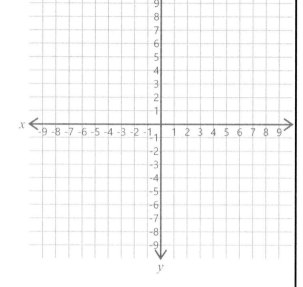

69. $y = \dfrac{-1}{2}x - 2$

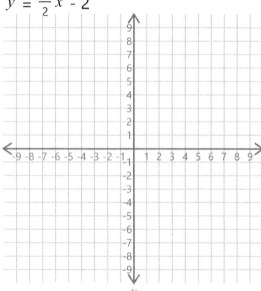

70. $y = -2x - 8$

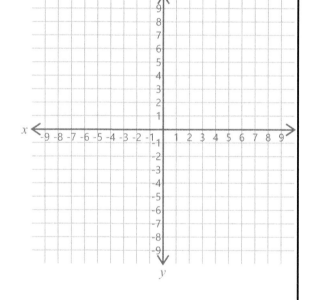

Slope-Intercept Form M1702-003

71. $y = -3x - 6$

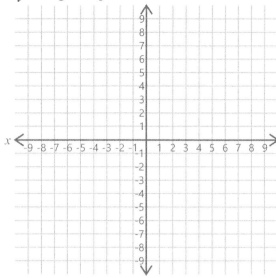

72. $y = \frac{1}{2}x - 9$

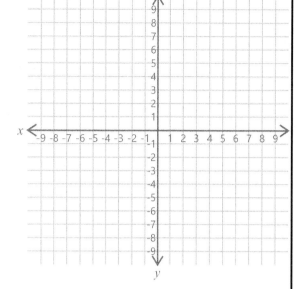

73. $y = \frac{-3}{4}x + 6$

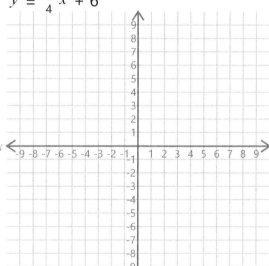

74. $y = \frac{5}{4}x - 9$

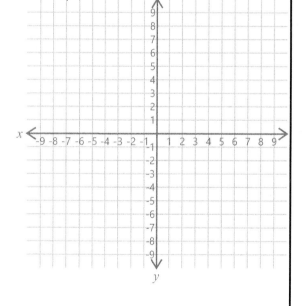

Slope-Intercept Form M1702-003

75. $x = 9$

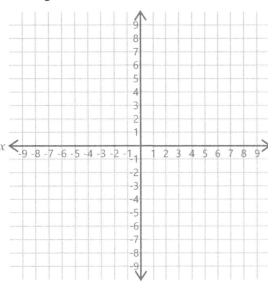

76. $y = \dfrac{-1}{2}x + 3$

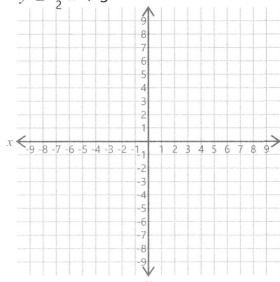

77. $y = \dfrac{-3}{2}x - 2$

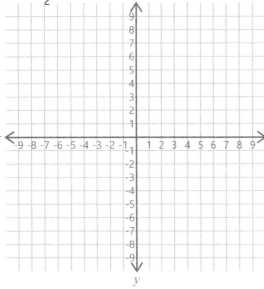

78. $y = 3x - 5$

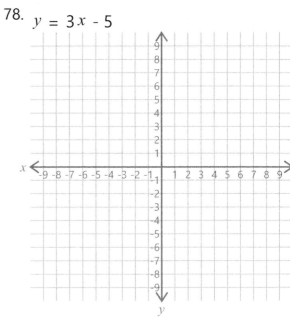

Slope-Intercept Form M1702-003

79. $y = -2x + 4$

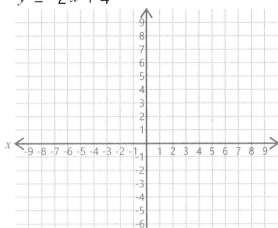

80. $y = \dfrac{-11}{4}x + 5$

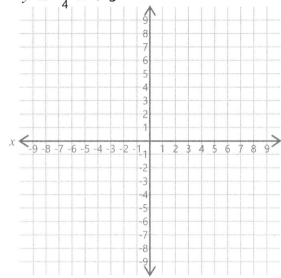

81. $y = \dfrac{1}{2}x + 9$

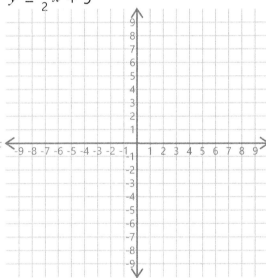

82. $y = \dfrac{5}{4}x + 8$

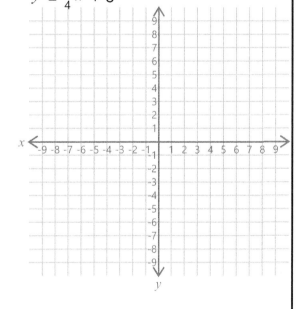

Slope-Intercept Form M1702-003

83. $y = \dfrac{-7}{4}x + 1$

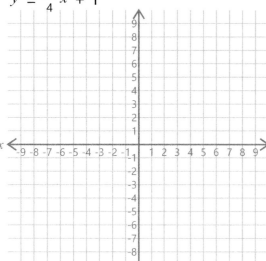

84. $y = 2x - 3$

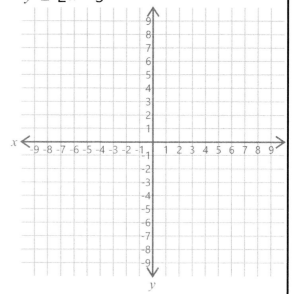

85. $y = 3x - 8$

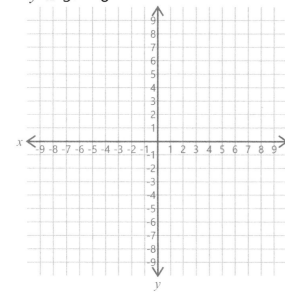

86. $y = \dfrac{-3}{2}x + 2$

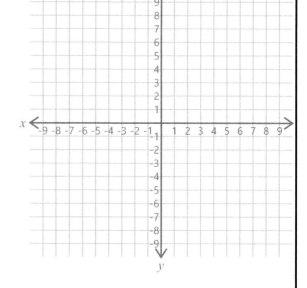

Slope-Intercept Form M1702-003

87. $y = \frac{1}{2}x - 5$

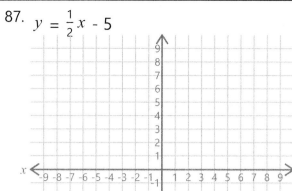

88. $y = \frac{9}{4}x + 4$

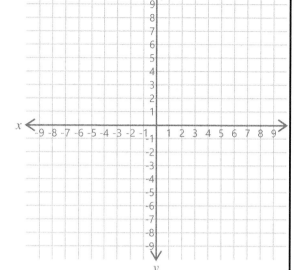

89. $y = -2x + 6$

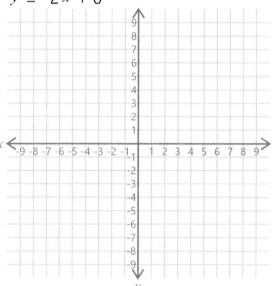

90. $y = \frac{1}{2}x - 6$

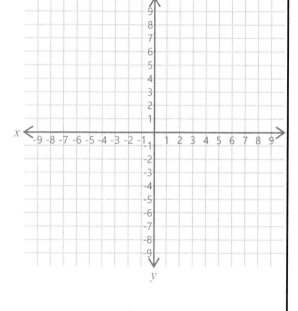

Slope-Intercept Form M1702-003

91. $y = \dfrac{11}{4}x - 6$

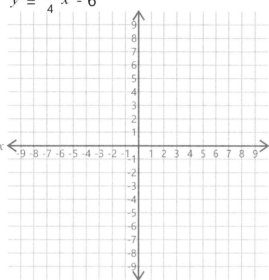

92. $y = \dfrac{-3}{4}x - 2$

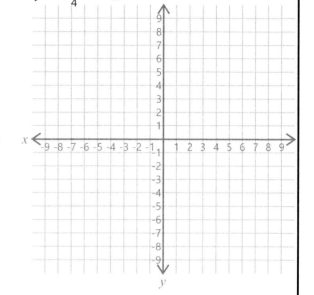

93. $y = \dfrac{3}{2}x - 6$

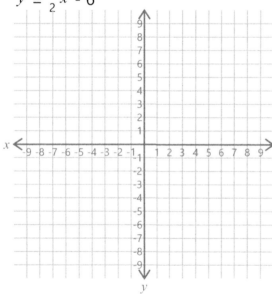

94. $y = x + 2$

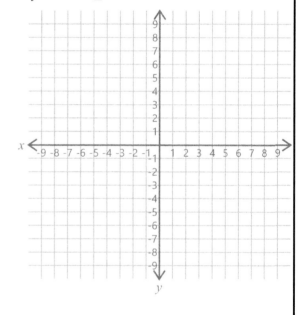

Slope-Intercept Form M1702-003

95. $y = \dfrac{-3}{2}x - 4$

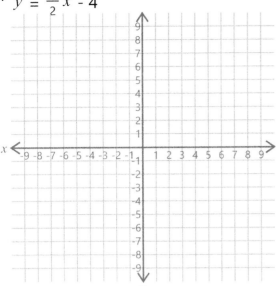

96. $y = \dfrac{-5}{2}x + 5$

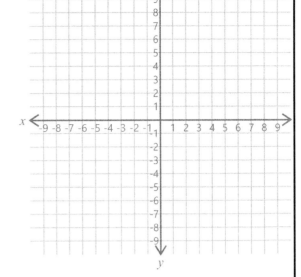

97. $y = 2x - 2$

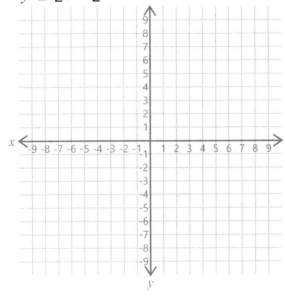

98. $y = \dfrac{-9}{4}x - 3$

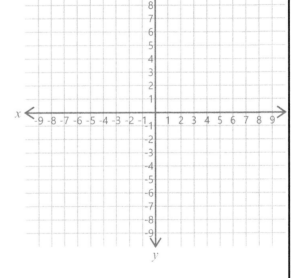

Slope-Intercept Form M1702-003

99. $y = \frac{1}{4}x + 6$

100. $y = 3x + 3$

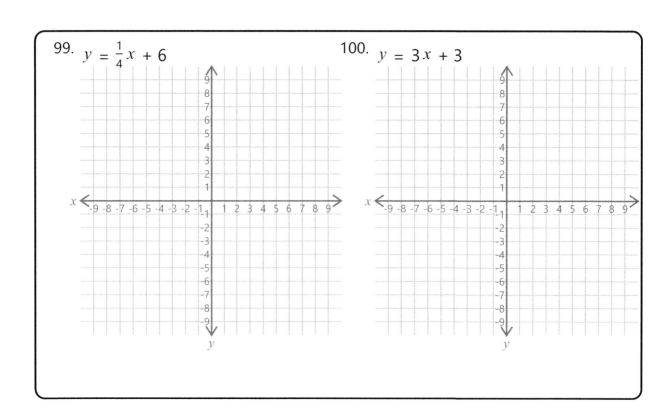

Name : _____ Date : _____

Timer : _____ Score : _____ / 100

Math Challenge

Slope-Intercept Form M1702-004

Draw the graph of each line.

1. $y = \dfrac{1}{2}x + 5$

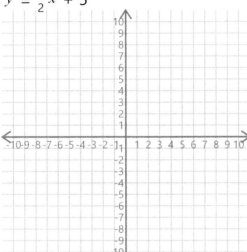

2. $y = \dfrac{3}{2}x + 1$

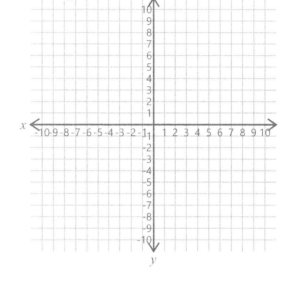

Slope-Intercept Form M1702-004

3. $y = \frac{-1}{4}x - 8$

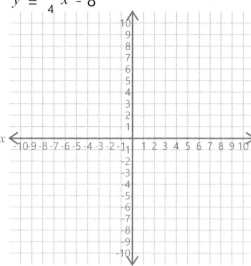

4. $y = \frac{3}{4}x - 10$

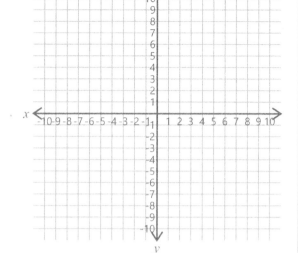

5. $y = \frac{-5}{2}x - 1$

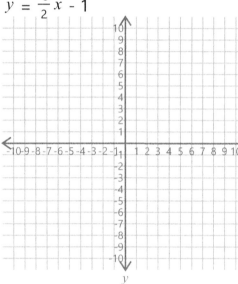

6. $y = \frac{-1}{2}x - 7$

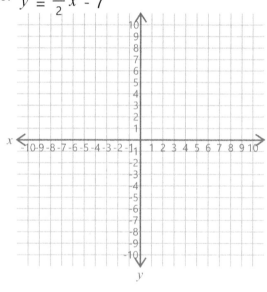

Slope-Intercept Form M1702-004

7. $x = 7$

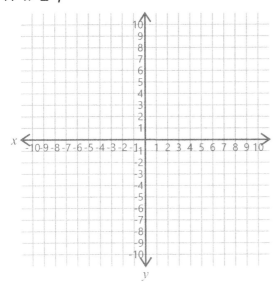

8. $y = \dfrac{5}{2}x + 1$

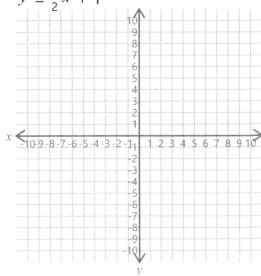

9. $y = \dfrac{-1}{4}x - 3$

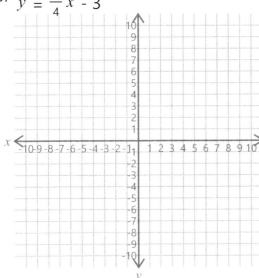

10. $y = \dfrac{-11}{4}x + 3$

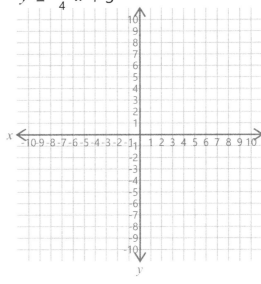

Slope-Intercept Form M1702-004

11. $y = 2x - 4$

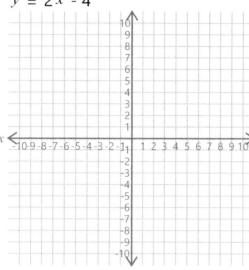

12. $y = \frac{1}{4}x - 7$

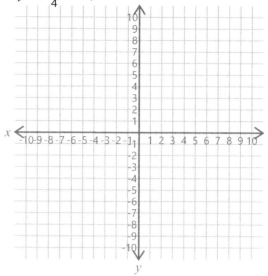

13. $y = \frac{5}{2}x - 4$

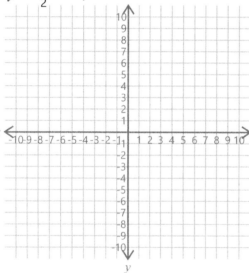

14. $y = -2x - 3$

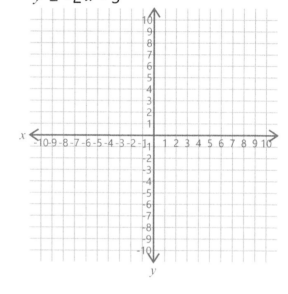

Slope-Intercept Form M1702-004

15. $y = \frac{7}{4}x - 7$

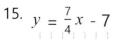

16. $y = -x - 4$

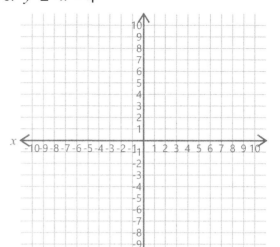

17. $y = -3x + 3$

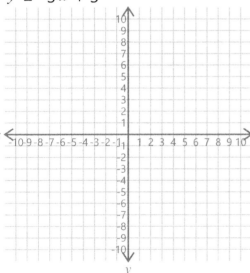

18. $y = 2x - 9$

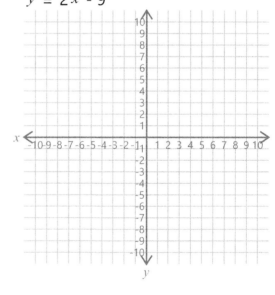

19. $y = \frac{-9}{4}x$

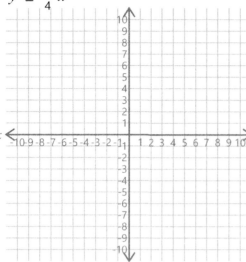

20. $y = \frac{-1}{4}x + 6$

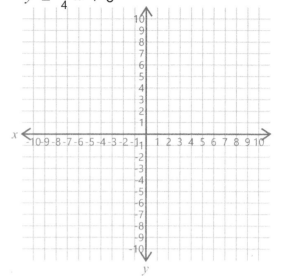

21. $y = x + 2$

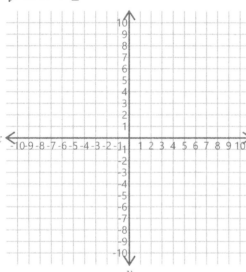

22. $y = \frac{-11}{4}x + 6$

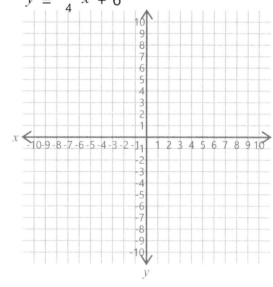

23. $y = \frac{-11}{4}x - 2$

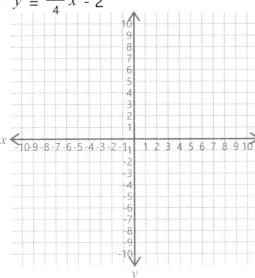

24. $x = -5$

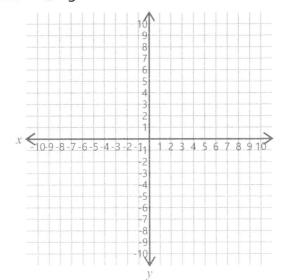

25. $y = \frac{-3}{4}x + 8$

26. $y = \frac{5}{4}x - 4$

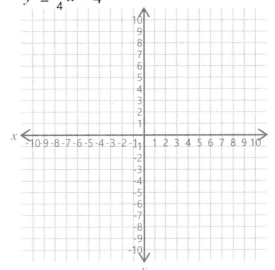

Slope-Intercept Form M1702-004

27. $y = \frac{3}{4}x + 5$

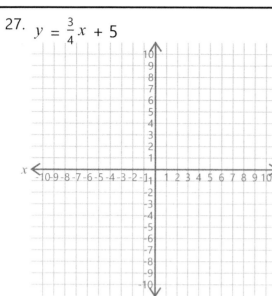

28. $y = \frac{3}{4}x - 5$

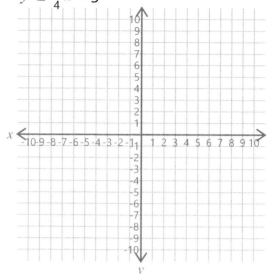

29. $y = \frac{-7}{4}x + 2$

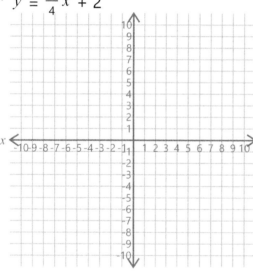

30. $y = \frac{5}{4}x - 8$

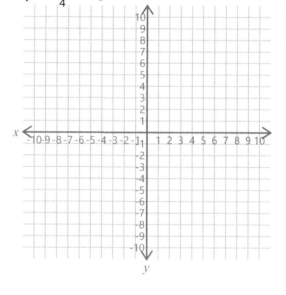

Slope-Intercept Form M1702-004

31. $y = 3x - 5$

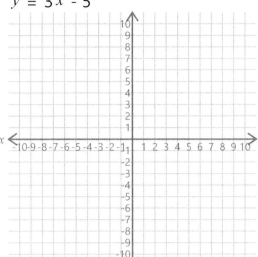

32. $y = \dfrac{-5}{4}x + 9$

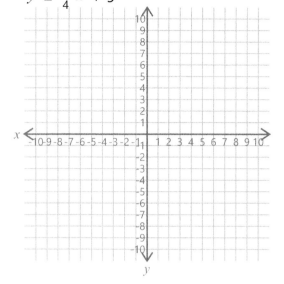

33. $y = \dfrac{-9}{4}x - 9$

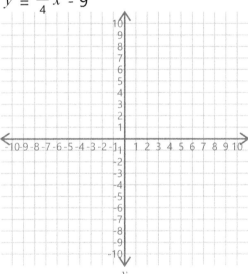

34. $y = -2x - 4$

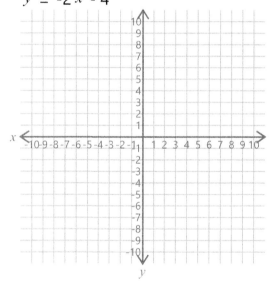

Slope-Intercept Form M1702-004

35. $y = \dfrac{-3}{4}x + 9$

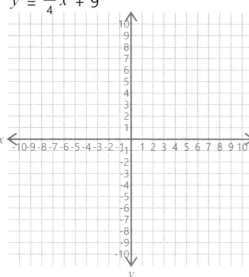

36. $x = -6$

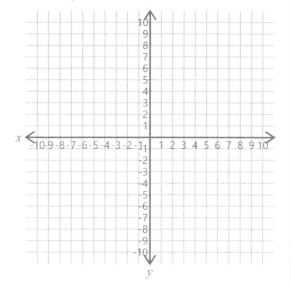

37. $y = \dfrac{-3}{2}x + 5$

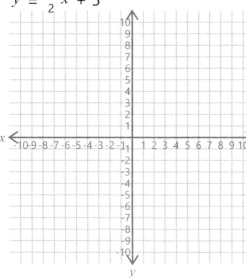

38. $y = -x + 9$

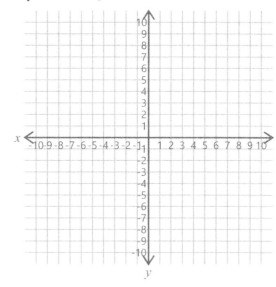

Slope-Intercept Form M1702-004

39. $x = 8$

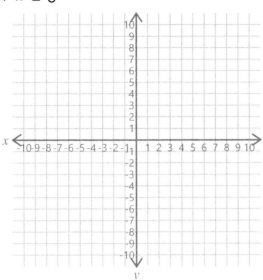

40. $y = \frac{1}{4}x - 10$

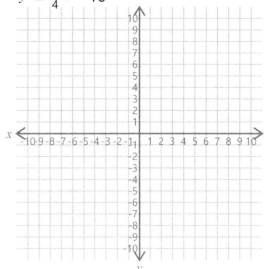

41. $y = \frac{7}{4}x - 4$

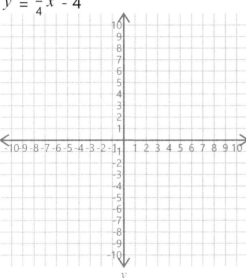

42. $y = \frac{-11}{4}x$

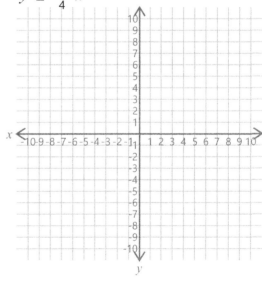

Slope-Intercept Form M1702-004

43. $y = \frac{5}{2}x + 2$

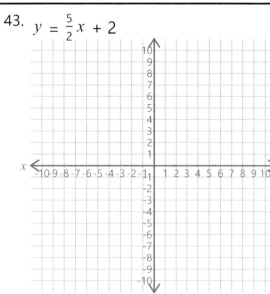

44. $y = \frac{9}{4}x - 3$

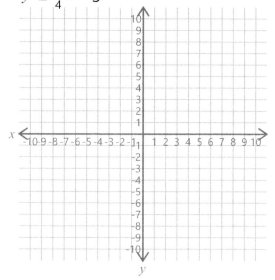

45. $y = \frac{-5}{4}x - 7$

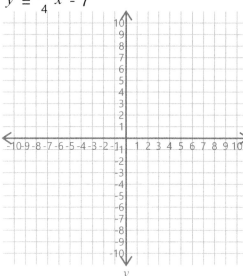

46. $y = \frac{5}{4}x + 10$

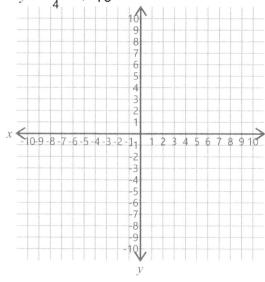

47. $y = \frac{-3}{2}x + 3$

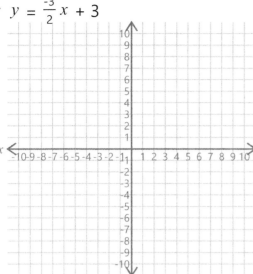

48. $y = -2x + 2$

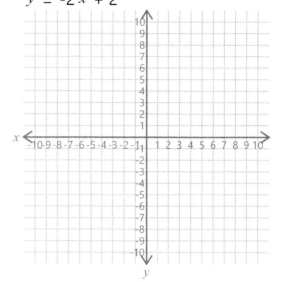

49. $y = \frac{1}{4}x + 4$

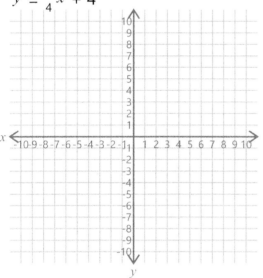

50. $y = \frac{-3}{4}x - 4$

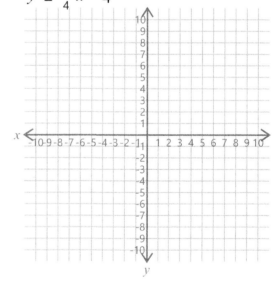

Slope-Intercept Form M1702-004

51. $y = \frac{3}{2}x - 2$

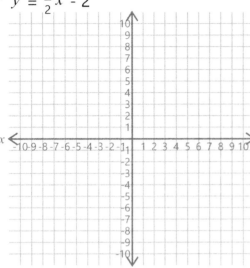

52. $y = -6$

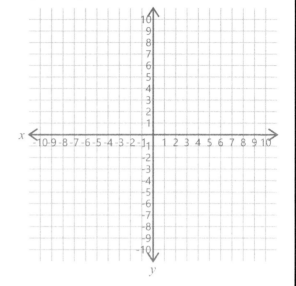

53. $y = 2x - 10$

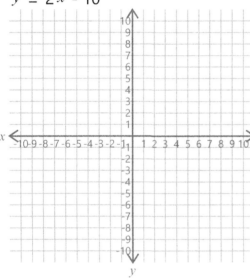

54. $y = \frac{-5}{4}x - 1$

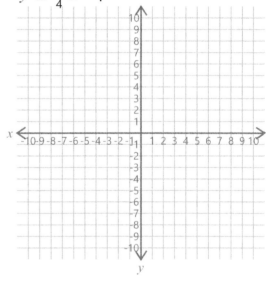

Slope-Intercept Form M1702-004

55. $y = \dfrac{-1}{2}x - 8$

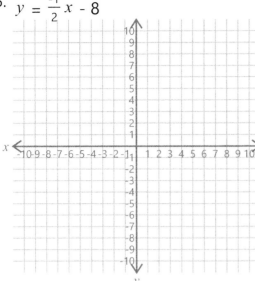

56. $y = -x + 8$

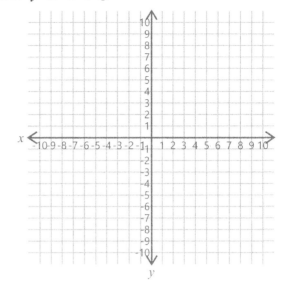

57. $y = \dfrac{-5}{4}x + 1$

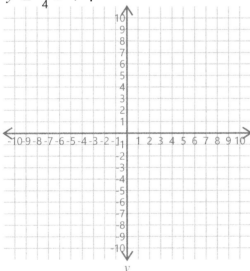

58. $y = 3x + 6$

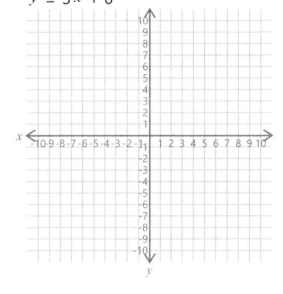

Slope-Intercept Form M1702-004

59. $y = \dfrac{-9}{4}x + 3$

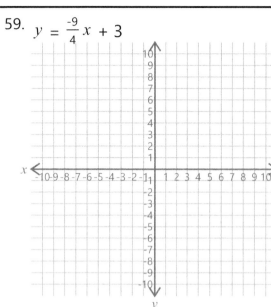

60. $y = \dfrac{-1}{4}x + 3$

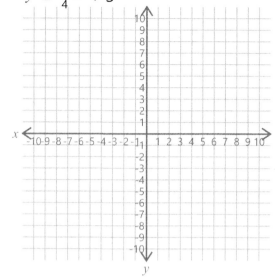

61. $y = \dfrac{11}{4}x - 9$

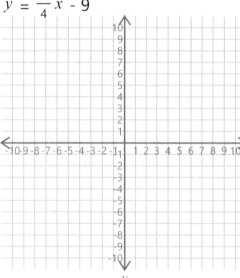

62. $y = \dfrac{-11}{4}x - 8$

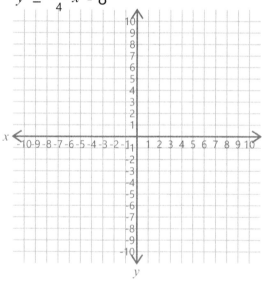

Slope-Intercept Form M1702-004

63. $y = \dfrac{-7}{4}x + 4$

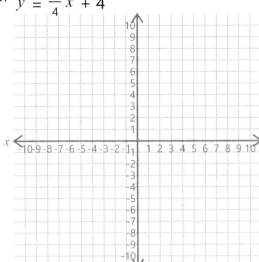

64. $y = \dfrac{7}{4}x - 2$

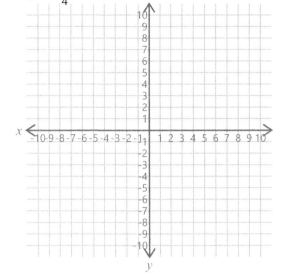

65. $y = \dfrac{-3}{4}x + 6$

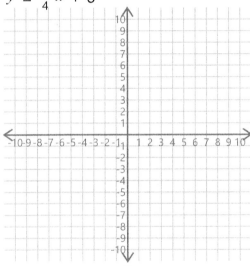

66. $y = \dfrac{5}{4}x - 2$

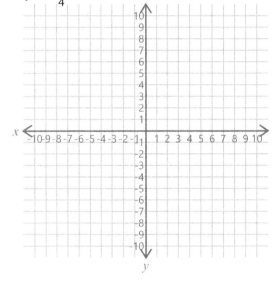

Slope-Intercept Form M1702-004

67. $y = \frac{3}{4}x + 3$

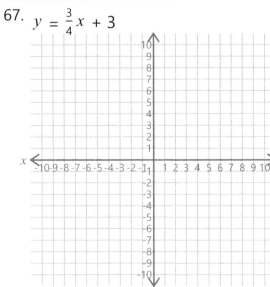

68. $y = \frac{-5}{2}x + 2$

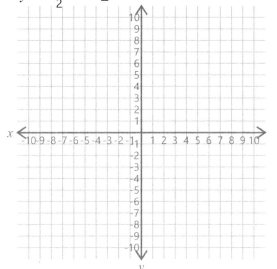

69. $y = \frac{1}{4}x + 6$

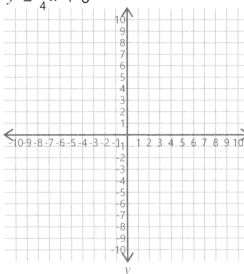

70. $y = \frac{-11}{4}x + 7$

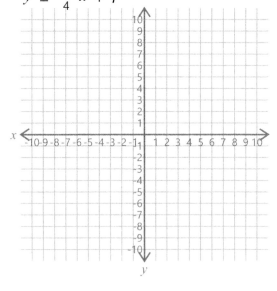

Slope-Intercept Form M1702-004

71. $y = \dfrac{7}{4}x + 1$

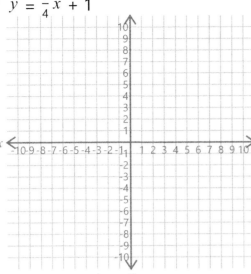

72. $y = x - 3$

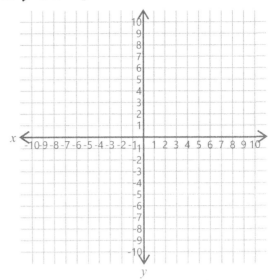

73. $y = \dfrac{-3}{4}x + 3$

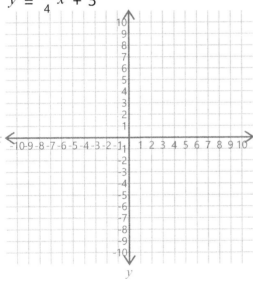

74. $y = x + 4$

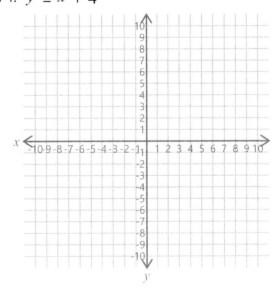

Slope-Intercept Form M1702-004

75. $y = \frac{5}{2}x - 8$

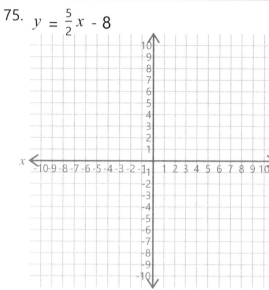

76. $y = + 10$

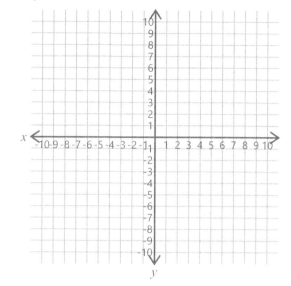

77. $y = -3x - 9$

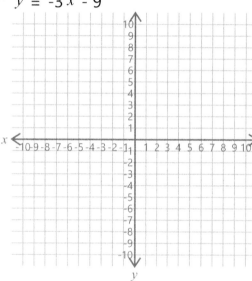

78. $y = \frac{-5}{4}x + 8$

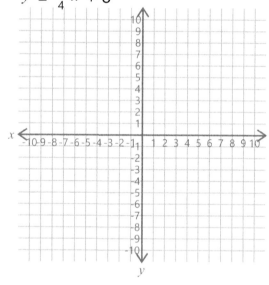

79. $y = \frac{-1}{4}x + 9$

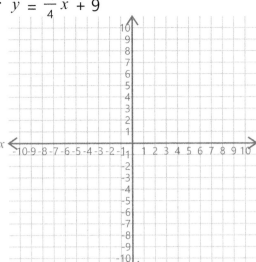

80. $y = \frac{-5}{4}x + 3$

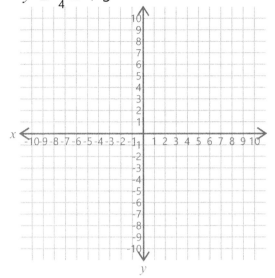

81. $y = \frac{5}{4}x + 1$

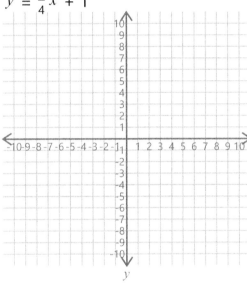

82. $y = \frac{-5}{2}x + 3$

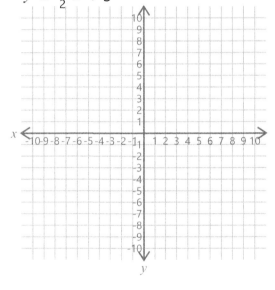

Slope-Intercept Form M1702-004

83. $y = \frac{1}{2}x - 9$

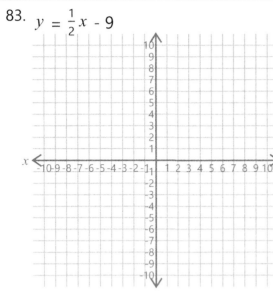

84. $y = -x + 1$

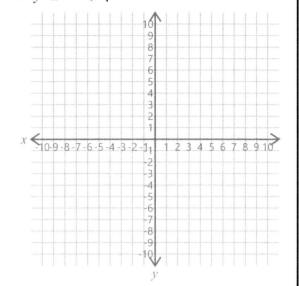

85. $y = \frac{1}{4}x + 7$

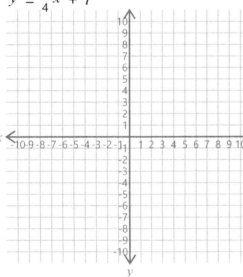

86. $y = -x - 8$

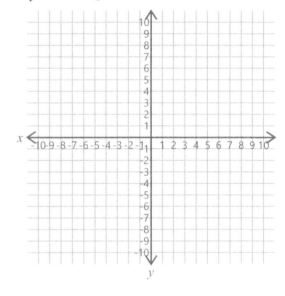

87. $y = \dfrac{7}{4}x + 3$

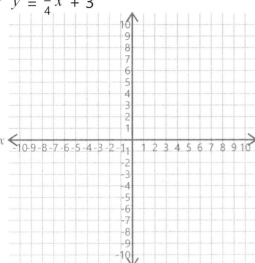

88. $y = \dfrac{-3}{2}x + 9$

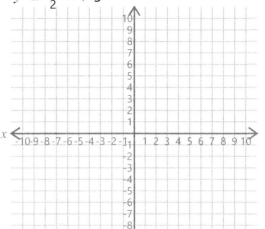

89. $y = \dfrac{1}{4}x$

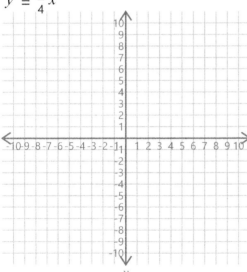

90. $y = \dfrac{3}{4}x - 1$

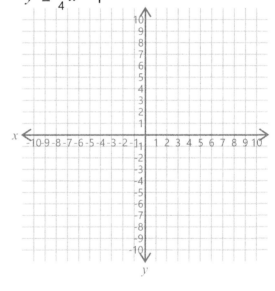

Slope-Intercept Form M1702-004

91. $y = 2x - 7$

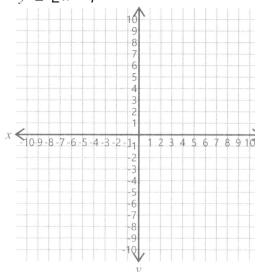

92. $y = \dfrac{-5}{2}x + 4$

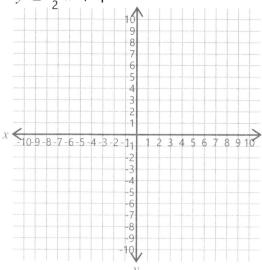

93. $y = \dfrac{-5}{2}x + 5$

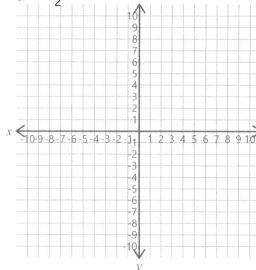

94. $y = -3x + 10$

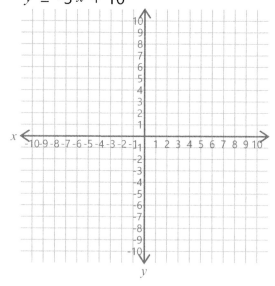

Slope-Intercept Form M1702-004

95. $y = \dfrac{1}{2}x - 1$

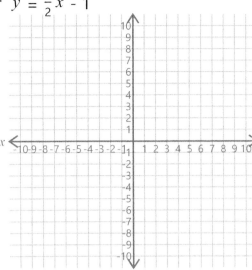

96. $y = \dfrac{5}{4}x + 8$

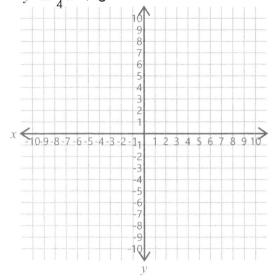

97. $y = \dfrac{9}{4}x - 7$

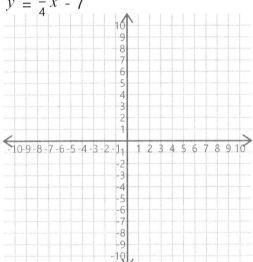

98. $y = \dfrac{-9}{4}x - 1$

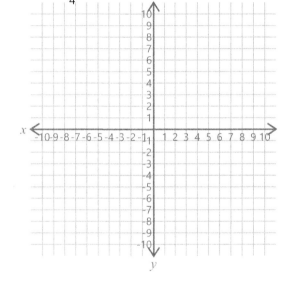

Slope-Intercept Form M1702-004

99. $y = -x$

100. $y = \dfrac{-1}{2}x + 7$

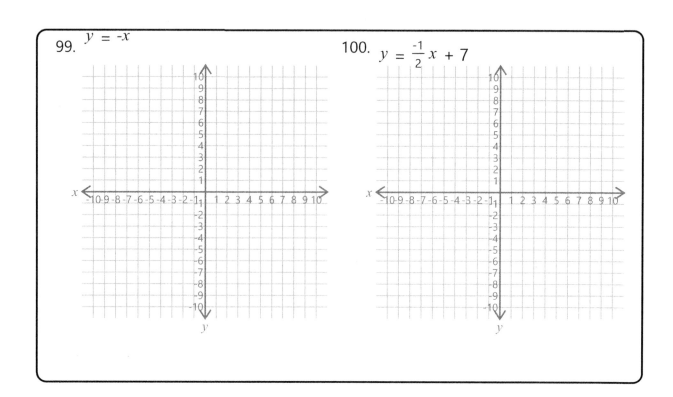

ANSWERS

Page 1: Slope-Intercept Form M1702-001

1. $y = -x + 7$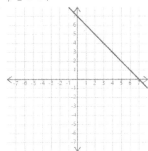

2. $y = \frac{3}{2}x - 2$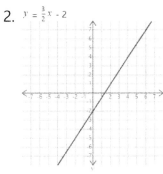

3. $y = \frac{1}{2}x + 6$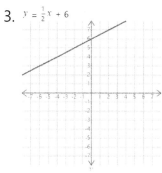

4. $y = \frac{9}{4}x + 6$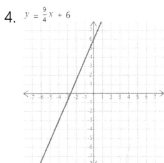

5. $y = -x + 5$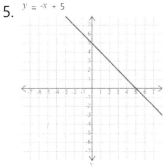

6. $y = x + 5$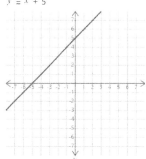

7. $y = \frac{-7}{4}x - 6$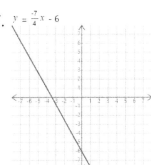

8. $y = \frac{1}{4}x$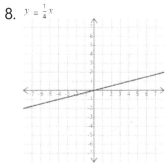

9. $y = \frac{1}{4}x + 3$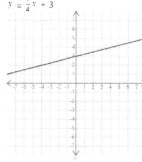

10. $y = \frac{1}{2}x - 7$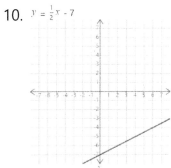

11. $y = 3x - 5$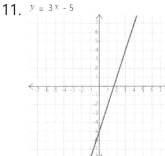

12. $y = \frac{-1}{4}x - 2$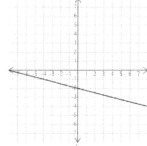

Slope-Intercept Form M1702-001

13. $y = \frac{-11}{4}x + 6$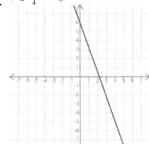

14. $y = \frac{-3}{2}x - 3$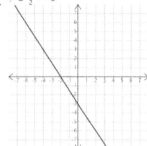

15. $y = \frac{3}{4}x - 1$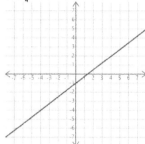

16. $y = \frac{-5}{4}x - 1$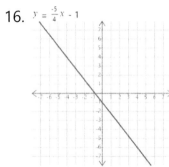

17. $y = x$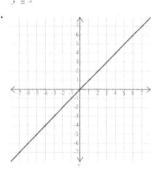

18. $y = \frac{-3}{2}x$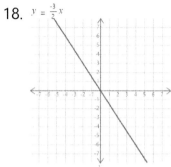

19. $y = -x + 6$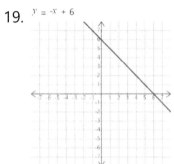

20. $y = \frac{1}{2}x + 3$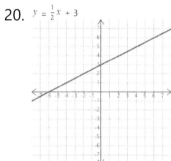

21. $y = \frac{-5}{2}x + 5$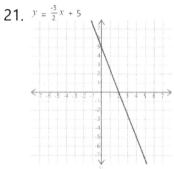

22. $y = 3x + 2$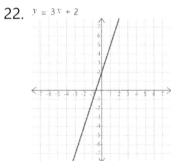

23. $y = \frac{-1}{2}x - 5$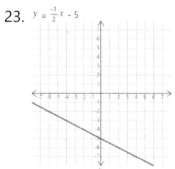

24. $y = x - 4$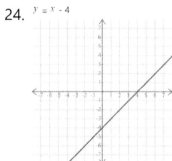

Slope-Intercept Form M1702-001

25. $y = -2x - 1$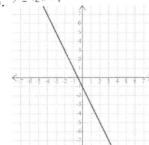

26. $y = \frac{-1}{2}x - 2$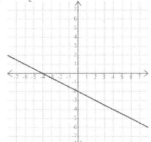

27. $y = \frac{9}{4}x - 3$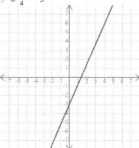

28. $y = \frac{-9}{4}x - 5$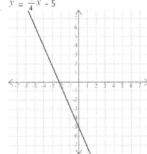

29. $y = \frac{1}{4}x - 2$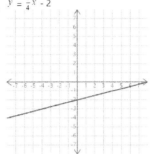

30. $y = \frac{-3}{4}x + 3$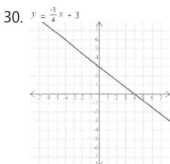

31. $y = \frac{-5}{4}x + 6$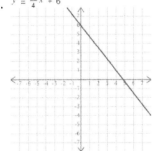

32. $y = \frac{1}{4}x - 4$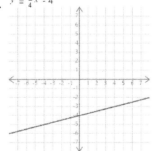

33. $y = -2x + 3$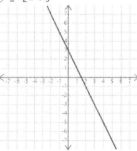

34. $y = \frac{5}{2}x + 7$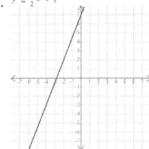

35. $y = -2x + 2$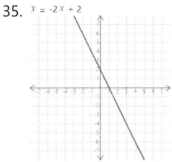

36. $y = -2x + 5$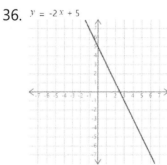

Slope-Intercept Form M1702-001

37. $y = \frac{11}{4}x - 6$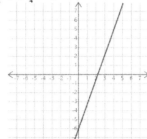

38. $y = -2x + 4$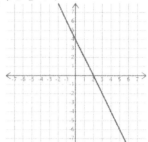

39. $y = 3x + 6$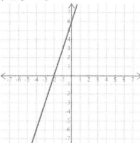

40. $y = \frac{-3}{2}x - 7$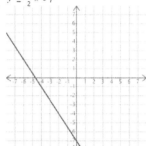

41. $y = x - 2$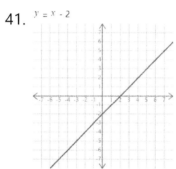

42. $y = \frac{-3}{4}x - 6$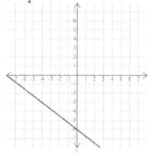

43. $y = -3x + 7$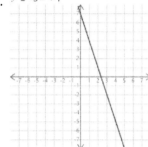

44. $y = \frac{-11}{4}x + 2$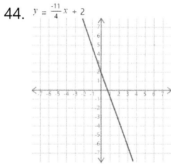

45. $y = \frac{-5}{2}x - 5$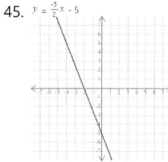

46. $x = 7$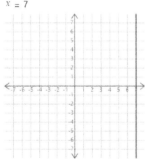

47. $y = \frac{-3}{4}x - 5$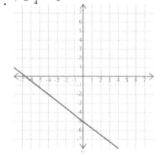

48. $y = \frac{-5}{4}x + 4$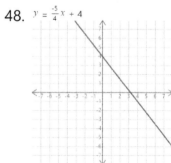

Slope-Intercept Form M1702-001

49. $y = \frac{-7}{4}x + 7$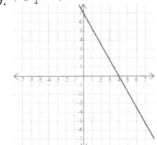

50. $y = \frac{-1}{2}x - 7$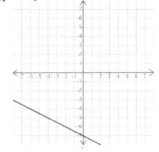

51. $x = 3$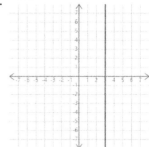

52. $y = \frac{-1}{4}x - 1$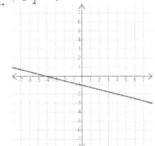

53. $y = \frac{-1}{4}x + 2$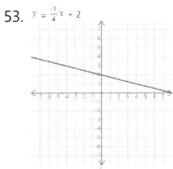

54. $y = \frac{9}{4}x + 2$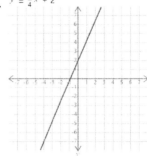

55. $y = \frac{3}{4}x + 5$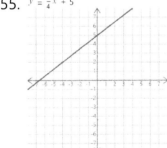

56. $x = -4$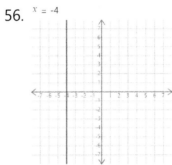

57. $y = \frac{-11}{4}x - 3$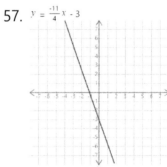

58. $y = \frac{1}{2}x - 6$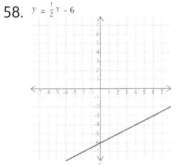

59. $y = \frac{5}{4}x + 4$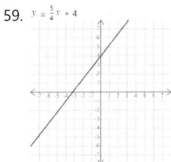

60. $y = 3x - 3$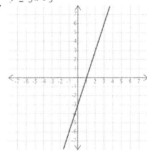

Slope-Intercept Form M1702-001

61. $y = x + 7$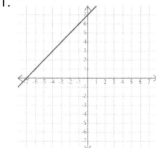

62. $y = \frac{11}{4}x - 4$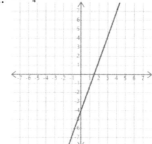

63. $y = \frac{3}{2}x + 2$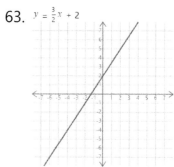

64. $y = 3x - 2$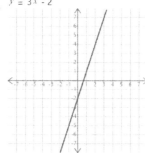

65. $y = \frac{-5}{2}x - 3$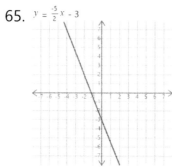

66. $y = -6$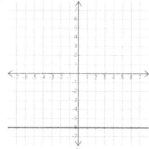

67. $y = \frac{-3}{2}x - 1$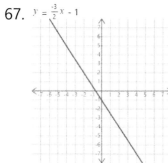

68. $y = \frac{-7}{4}x$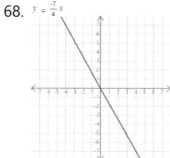

69. $y = \frac{3}{4}x - 5$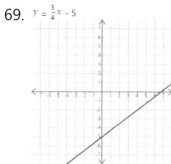

70. $y = x + 2$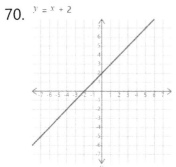

71. $y = -2x - 7$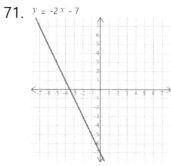

72. $y = \frac{7}{4}x + 6$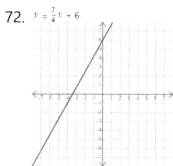

Slope-Intercept Form M1702-001

73. $y = \frac{-9}{4}x - 6$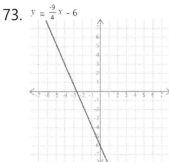

74. $y = \frac{-1}{4}x + 6$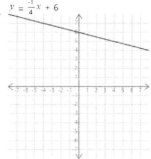

75. $y = \frac{-11}{4}x + 3$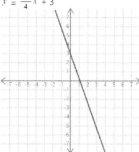

76. $y = \frac{1}{4}x - 6$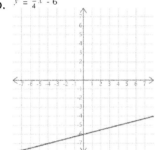

77. $y = \frac{-7}{4}x + 1$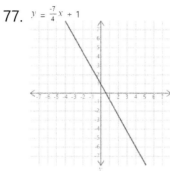

78. $y = \frac{11}{4}x + 6$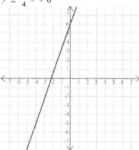

79. $y = \frac{3}{2}x + 3$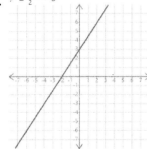

80. $y = \frac{3}{2}x + 7$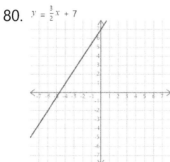

81. $y = \frac{5}{2}x - 2$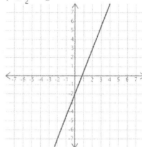

82. $y = \frac{-11}{4}x - 6$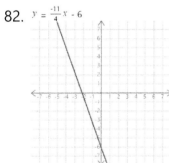

83. $y = \frac{11}{4}x - 5$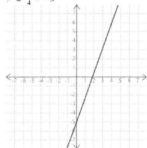

84. $y = \frac{-9}{4}x + 4$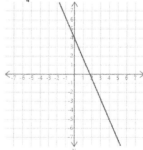

Slope-Intercept Form M1702-001

85. $y = \frac{3}{2}x - 7$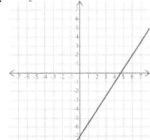

86. $y = \frac{9}{4}x + 5$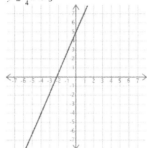

87. $y = \frac{1}{4}x + 5$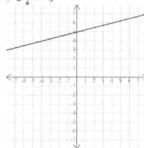

88. $y = \frac{-3}{2}x + 5$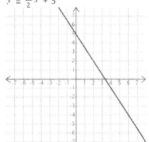

89. $y = \frac{3}{4}x - 2$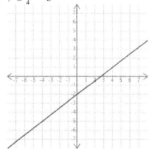

90. $y = +6$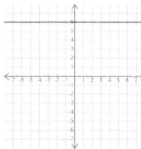

91. $y = \frac{-3}{2}x + 2$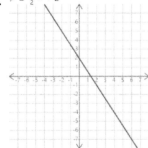

92. $y = \frac{3}{4}x + 3$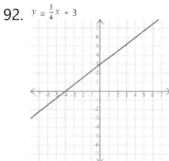

93. $y = \frac{-3}{2}x + 3$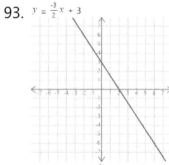

94. $y = \frac{11}{4}x - 1$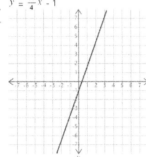

95. $y = -x + 4$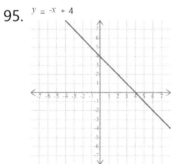

96. $y = \frac{-11}{4}x + 4$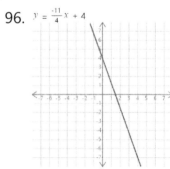

Slope-Intercept Form M1702-001

97. $y = -3x - 2$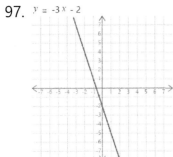

98. $x = 5$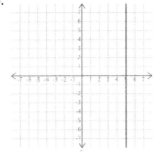

99. $y = \frac{-1}{2}x + 6$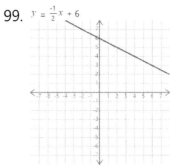

100. $y = \frac{1}{2}x - 2$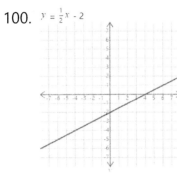

Slope-Intercept Form M1702-001

ANSWERS

Page 1: Slope-Intercept Form M1702-002

1. $y = \frac{3}{4}x - 5$
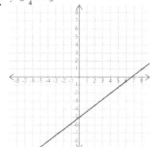

2. $y = -3x$
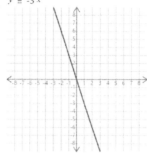

3. $y = \frac{-1}{2}x - 4$
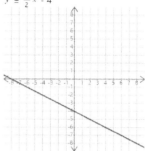

4. $y = \frac{-1}{2}x + 8$
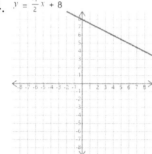

5. $y = -2x - 8$
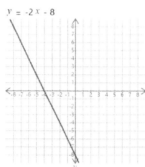

6. $y = \frac{5}{4}x + 2$
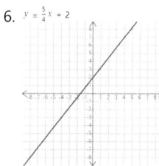

7. $y = \frac{-1}{2}x$
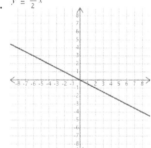

8. $y = \frac{7}{4}x + 7$
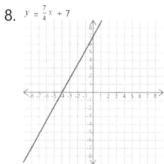

9. $x = 2$
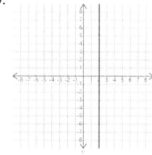

10. $y = \frac{-3}{4}x + 6$
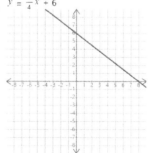

11. $y = 2x$
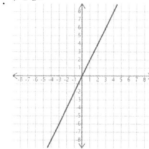

12. $y = \frac{-3}{4}x - 5$
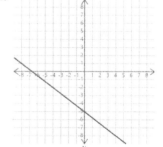

Slope-Intercept Form M1702-002

13. $y = \frac{-1}{4}x + 6$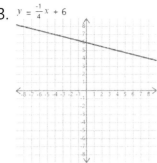

14. $y = \frac{-7}{4}x + 2$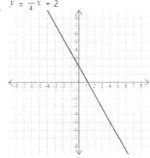

15. $y = \frac{-3}{2}x + 2$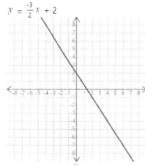

16. $y = \frac{7}{4}x - 2$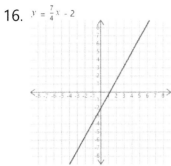

17. $y = \frac{5}{2}x - 1$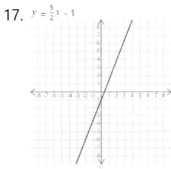

18. $y = \frac{5}{4}x - 2$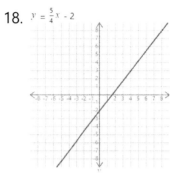

19. $y = \frac{7}{4}x$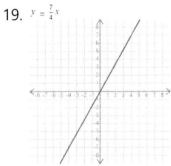

20. $y = -8$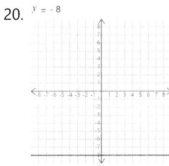

21. $y = \frac{-3}{2}x - 3$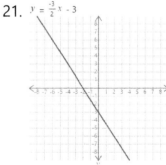

22. $y = \frac{1}{4}x - 3$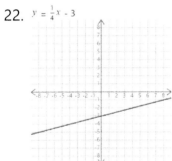

23. $y = -2x - 4$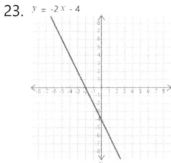

24. $y = \frac{-7}{4}x - 8$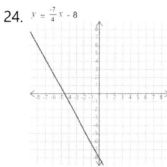

Slope-Intercept Form M1702-002

25. $y = \frac{11}{4}x - 5$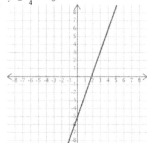

26. $y = \frac{3}{2}x - 5$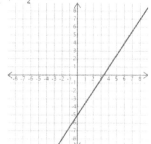

27. $y = -x + 4$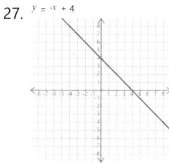

28. $y = \frac{-3}{4}x - 6$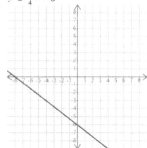

29. $y = \frac{9}{4}x + 5$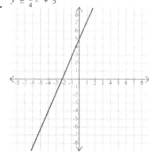

30. $y = \frac{-11}{4}x + 1$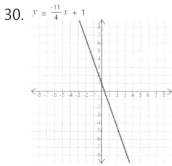

31. $y = \frac{-11}{4}x + 5$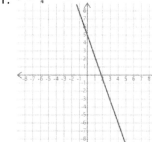

32. $y = \frac{3}{2}x + 2$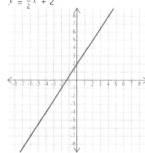

33. $y = 2x + 8$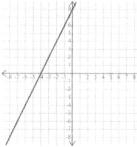

34. $y = \frac{9}{4}x - 2$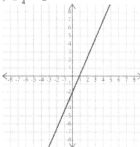

35. $y = -2x$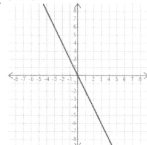

36. $y = -2x - 3$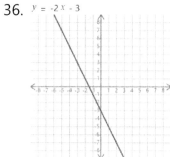

Slope-Intercept Form M1702-002

37. $y = \frac{3}{4}x$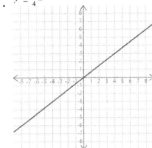

38. $x = -7$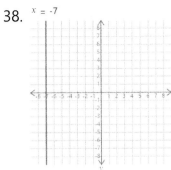

39. $y = -3x - 5$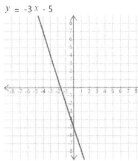

40. $y = x - 5$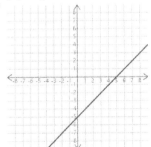

41. $y = \frac{7}{4}x - 8$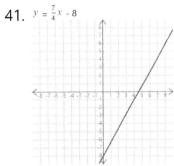

42. $y = \frac{5}{2}x + 1$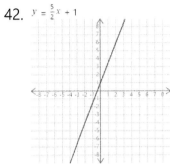

43. $y = \frac{-11}{4}x - 6$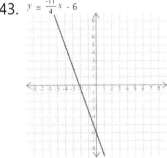

44. $y = \frac{-5}{2}x + 1$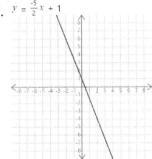

45. $y = \frac{1}{4}x + 7$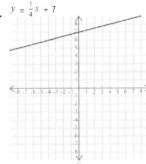

46. $y = \frac{-1}{2}x + 7$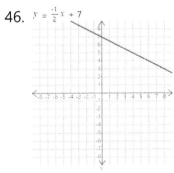

47. $x = 0$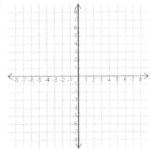

48. $y = \frac{3}{4}x + 7$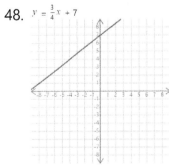

Slope-Intercept Form M1702-002

49. $y = \frac{-11}{4}x + 6$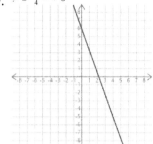

50. $y = \frac{-1}{4}x - 4$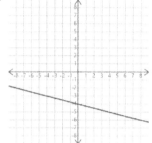

51. $y = \frac{-11}{4}x - 5$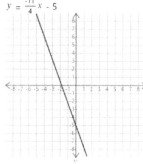

52. $y = \frac{-11}{4}x + 8$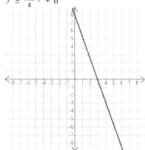

53. $y = \frac{-9}{4}x + 6$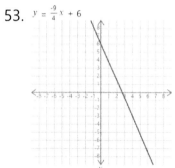

54. $y = \frac{-9}{4}x + 5$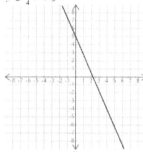

55. $y = 2x + 6$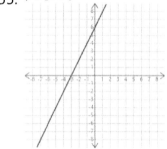

56. $y = 3x + 6$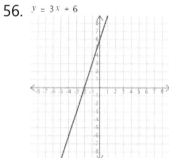

57. $y = -3x + 3$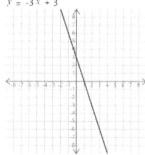

58. $y = \frac{3}{2}x + 3$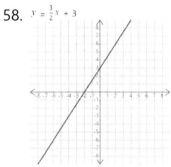

59. $y = \frac{-3}{2}x + 3$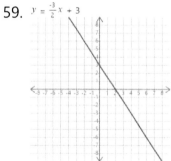

60. $y = \frac{5}{2}x - 4$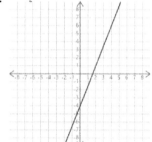

Slope-Intercept Form M1702-002

61. $y = \frac{5}{2}x - 5$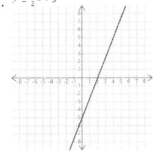

62. $y = \frac{-11}{4}x - 4$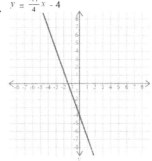

63. $y = -x - 7$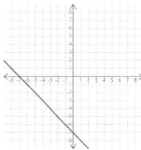

64. $y = \frac{11}{4}x - 8$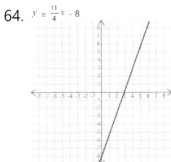

65. $y = -3x - 6$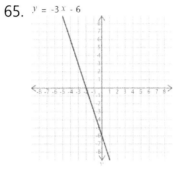

66. $x = 3$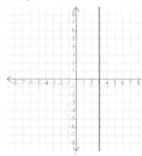

67. $y = -7$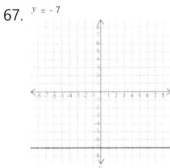

68. $y = \frac{-1}{2}x + 4$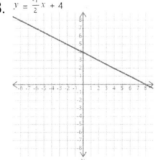

69. $y = \frac{-9}{4}x + 1$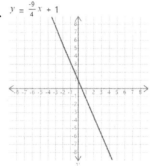

70. $x = -6$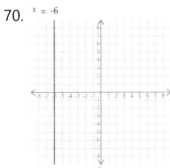

71. $y = \frac{-1}{4}x + 7$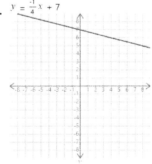

72. $y = \frac{-7}{4}x - 2$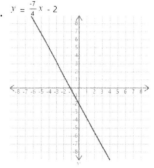

Slope-Intercept Form M1702-002

73. $y = x + 5$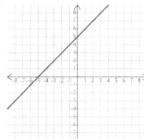

74. $y = x + 6$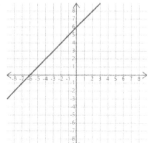

75. $y = -2x + 5$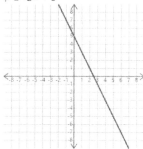

76. $y = \frac{5}{4}x - 8$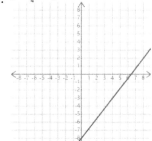

77. $y = 2x + 2$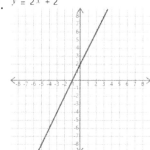

78. $y = 2x + 5$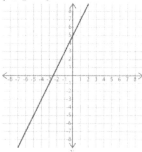

79. $y = \frac{3}{2}x - 7$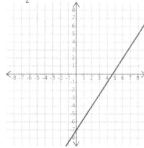

80. $y = \frac{-7}{4}x - 6$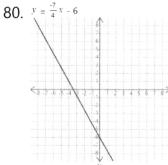

81. $y = x + 3$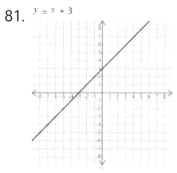

82. $y = \frac{5}{2}x - 6$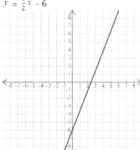

83. $y = \frac{-5}{2}x$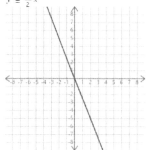

84. $y = \frac{-5}{4}x - 5$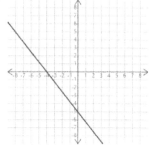

Slope-Intercept Form M1702-002

85. $y = x + 8$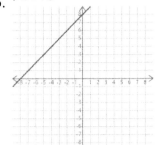

86. $y = \frac{9}{4}x + 3$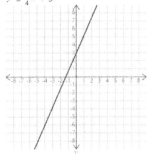

87. $y = \frac{1}{4}x + 8$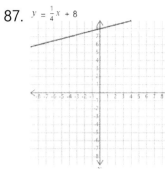

88. $y = \frac{3}{4}x - 6$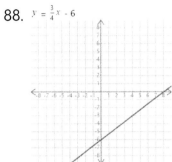

89. $y = +3$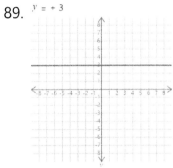

90. $y = \frac{-7}{4}x - 3$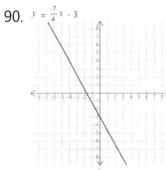

91. $y = \frac{-1}{4}x - 1$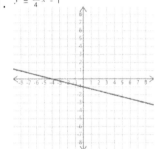

92. $y = \frac{-3}{4}x + 2$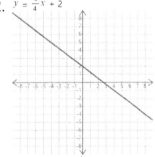

93. $y = -2x - 6$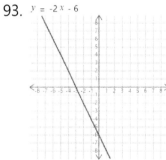

94. $y = \frac{-9}{4}x - 1$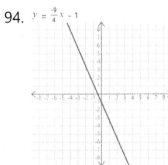

95. $y = \frac{-9}{4}x + 4$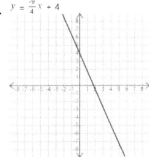

96. $y = \frac{-11}{4}x$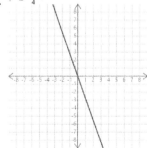

Slope-Intercept Form M1702-002

97. $y = \frac{7}{4}x + 2$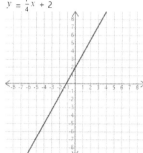

98. $y = \frac{1}{2}x$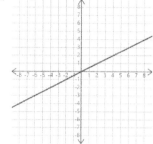

99. $y = \frac{-1}{2}x - 8$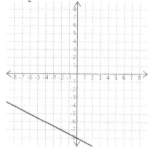

100. $y = \frac{-5}{4}x - 6$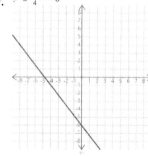

ANSWERS

Page 1: Slope-Intercept Form M1702-003

1. $y = \frac{-3}{2}x + 1$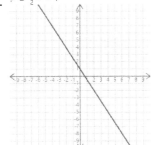
2. $y = \frac{-3}{4}x - 4$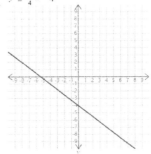
3. $y = -3x + 4$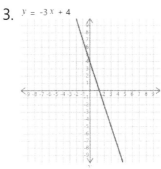
4. $y = \frac{-1}{4}x + 5$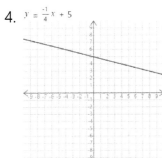
5. $y = \frac{5}{2}x - 8$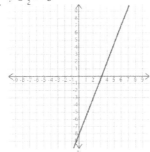
6. $y = \frac{-5}{4}x + 6$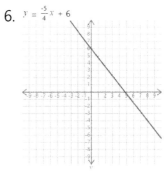
7. $y = -x + 2$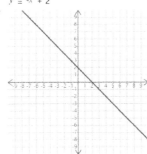
8. $y = \frac{9}{4}x + 9$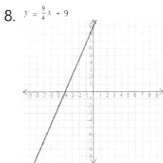
9. $y = \frac{3}{2}x - 4$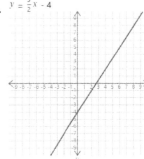
10. $y = \frac{3}{4}x - 9$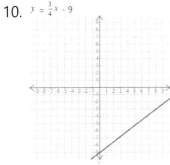
11. $y = \frac{-5}{4}x + 3$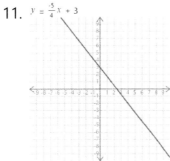
12. $y = \frac{9}{4}x - 4$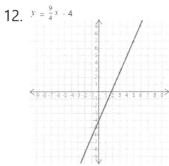

13. $y = \frac{-3}{2}x - 9$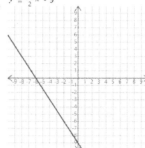

14. $y = \frac{-5}{4}x - 6$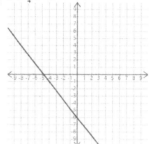

15. $y = -3x + 9$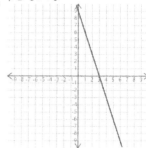

16. $y = \frac{-5}{2}x - 5$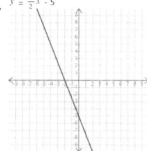

17. $y = \frac{1}{2}x + 6$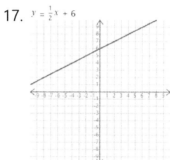

18. $y = \frac{-5}{2}x + 3$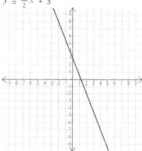

19. $y = +8$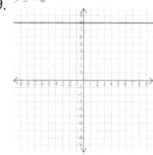

20. $y = 3x + 1$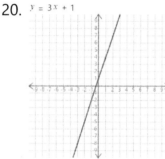

21. $y = \frac{5}{2}x - 2$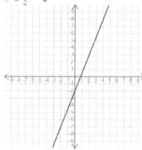

22. $y = \frac{-1}{4}x$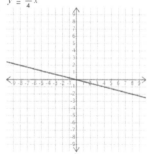

23. $y = \frac{5}{2}x + 7$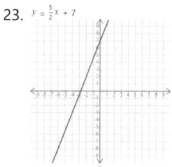

24. $y = -2x - 9$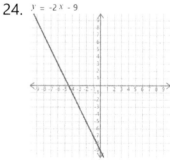

Slope-Intercept Form M1702-003

25. $y = x + 3$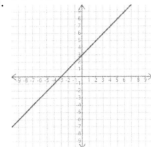

26. $y = \frac{7}{4}x + 6$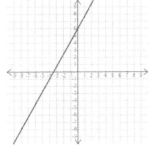

27. $y = \frac{1}{2}x + 4$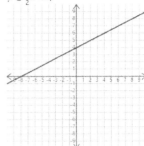

28. $y = \frac{1}{2}x + 3$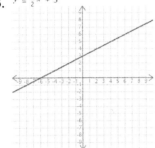

29. $y = \frac{3}{2}x - 8$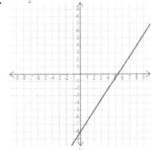

30. $y = \frac{-11}{4}x - 9$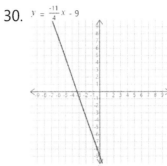

31. $y = \frac{-1}{2}x - 4$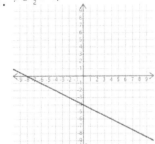

32. $y = \frac{7}{4}x + 7$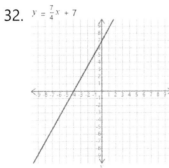

33. $x = -9$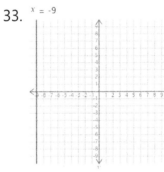

34. $y = \frac{-3}{2}x$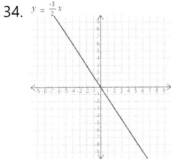

35. $y = \frac{1}{4}x - 6$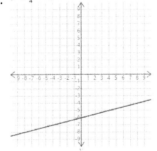

36. $y = + 6$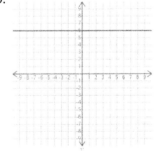

37. $y = \frac{-5}{4}x - 8$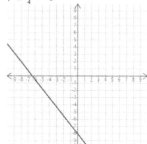

38. $y = \frac{-9}{4}x + 8$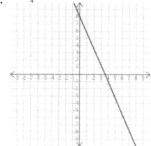

39. $y = \frac{-7}{4}x - 4$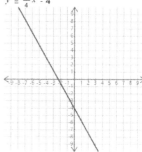

40. $y = \frac{-1}{4}x - 3$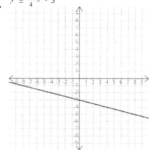

41. $y = \frac{5}{2}x - 5$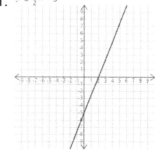

42. $y = \frac{1}{4}x - 3$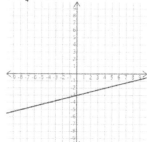

43. $y = x + 6$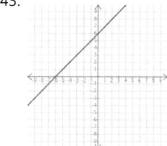

44. $y = \frac{-3}{2}x - 1$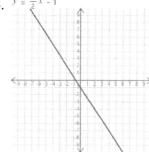

45. $y = \frac{11}{4}x - 2$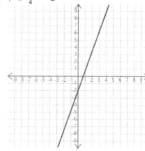

46. $y = \frac{-9}{4}x + 2$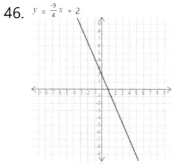

47. $y = x + 1$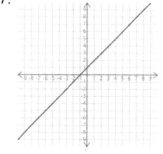

48. $y = \frac{1}{4}x - 1$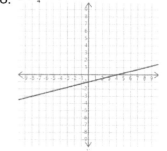

49. $y = -2x + 9$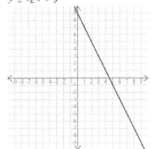

50. $y = \frac{1}{4}x$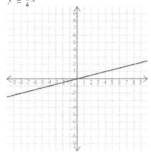

51. $y = \frac{-1}{4}x - 1$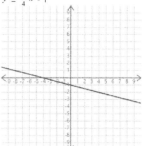

52. $y = x + 4$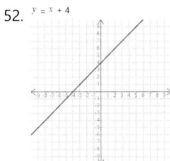

53. $y = \frac{-9}{4}x - 6$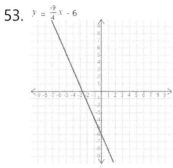

54. $y = \frac{7}{4}x - 1$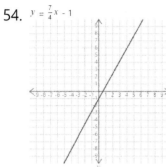

55. $y = \frac{-1}{2}x - 1$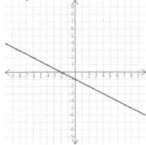

56. $y = \frac{-3}{2}x - 8$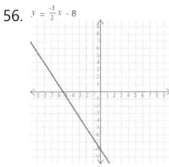

57. $y = \frac{-5}{4}x - 7$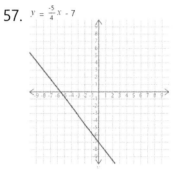

58. $y = 3x - 3$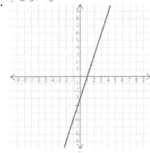

59. $y = \frac{7}{4}x + 3$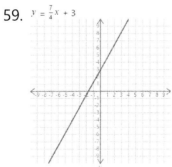

60. $y = \frac{7}{4}x - 6$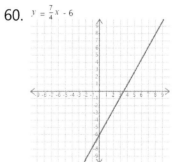

Slope-Intercept Form M1702-003

61. $y = \frac{7}{4}x - 8$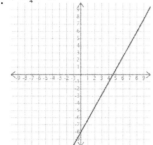

62. $y = -2x - 5$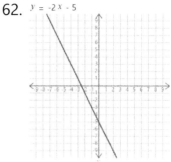

63. $y = \frac{7}{4}x - 7$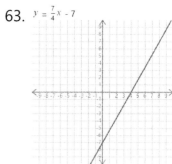

64. $y = -3x$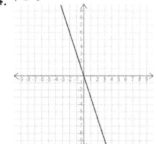

65. $y = 2x + 9$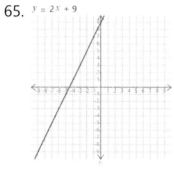

66. $y = \frac{9}{4}x - 6$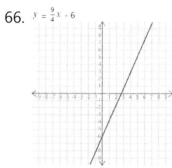

67. $y = 3x + 7$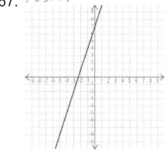

68. $y = \frac{-1}{2}x - 6$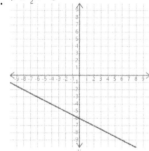

69. $y = \frac{-1}{2}x - 2$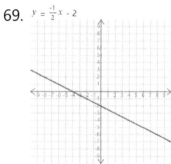

70. $y = -2x - 8$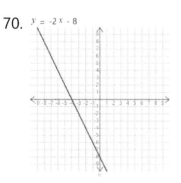

71. $y = -3x - 6$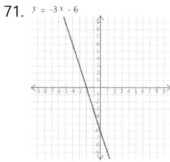

72. $y = \frac{1}{2}x - 9$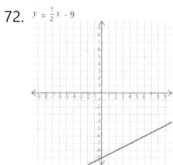

Slope-Intercept Form M1702-003

73. $y = \frac{-3}{4}x + 6$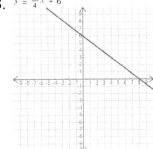

74. $y = \frac{5}{4}x - 9$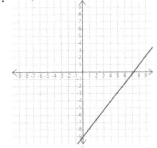

75. $x = 9$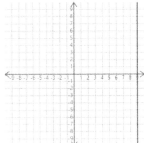

76. $y = \frac{-1}{2}x + 3$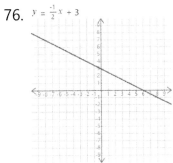

77. $y = \frac{-3}{2}x - 2$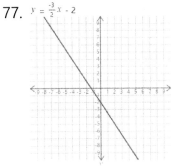

78. $y = 3x - 5$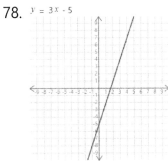

79. $y = -2x + 4$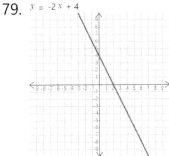

80. $y = \frac{-11}{4}x + 5$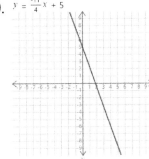

81. $y = \frac{1}{2}x + 9$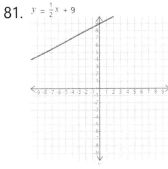

82. $y = \frac{5}{4}x + 8$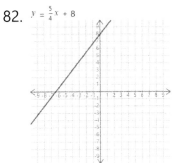

83. $y = \frac{-7}{4}x + 1$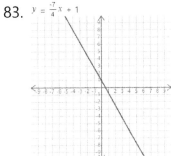

84. $y = 2x - 3$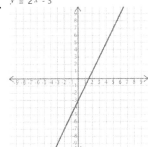

Slope-Intercept Form M1702-003

85. $y = 3x - 8$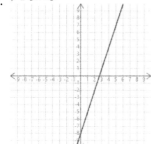

86. $y = \frac{-3}{2}x + 2$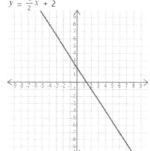

87. $y = \frac{1}{2}x - 5$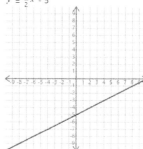

88. $y = \frac{9}{4}x + 4$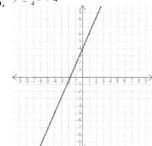

89. $y = -2x + 6$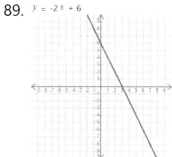

90. $y = \frac{1}{2}x - 6$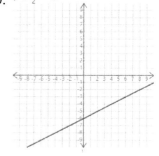

91. $y = \frac{11}{4}x - 6$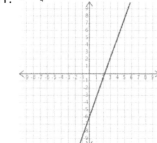

92. $y = \frac{-3}{4}x - 2$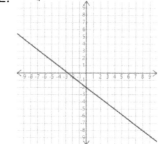

93. $y = \frac{3}{2}x - 6$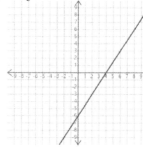

94. $y = x + 2$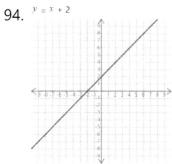

95. $y = \frac{-3}{2}x - 4$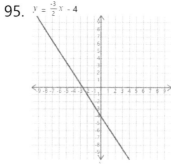

96. $y = \frac{-5}{2}x + 5$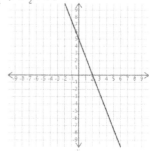

Slope-Intercept Form M1702-003

97. $y = 2x - 2$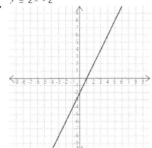

98. $y = \frac{-9}{4}x - 3$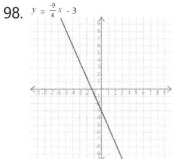

99. $y = \frac{1}{4}x + 6$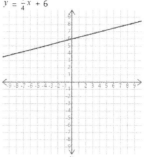

100. $y = 3x + 3$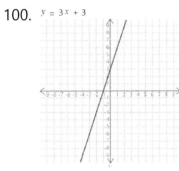

Slope-Intercept Form M1702-003

ANSWERS

Page 1: Slope-Intercept Form M1702-004

1. $y = \frac{1}{2}x + 5$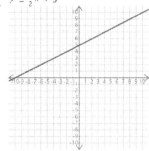

2. $y = \frac{3}{2}x + 1$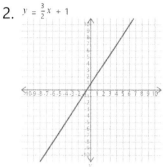

3. $y = \frac{-1}{4}x - 8$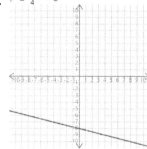

4. $y = \frac{3}{4}x - 10$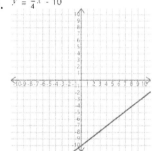

5. $y = \frac{-5}{2}x - 1$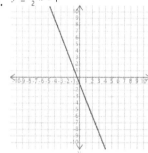

6. $y = \frac{-1}{2}x - 7$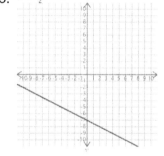

7. $x = 7$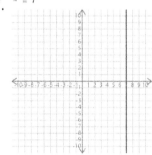

8. $y = \frac{5}{2}x + 1$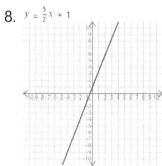

9. $y = \frac{-1}{4}x - 3$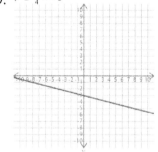

10. $y = \frac{-11}{4}x + 3$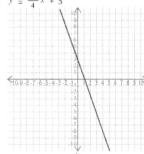

11. $y = 2x - 4$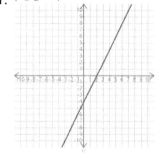

12. $y = \frac{1}{4}x - 7$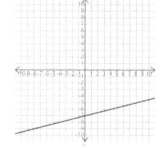

13. $y = \frac{5}{2}x - 4$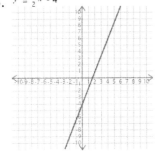

14. $y = -2x - 3$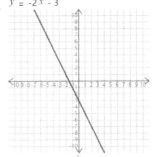

15. $y = \frac{7}{4}x - 7$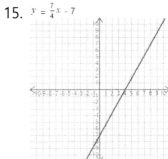

16. $y = -x - 4$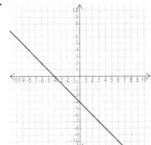

17. $y = -3x + 3$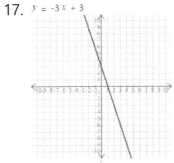

18. $y = 2x - 9$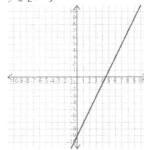

19. $y = \frac{-9}{4}x$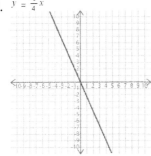

20. $y = \frac{-1}{4}x + 6$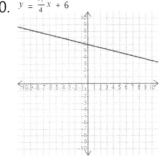

21. $y = x + 2$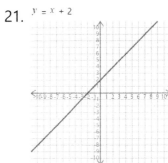

22. $y = \frac{-11}{4}x + 6$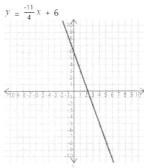

23. $y = \frac{-11}{4}x - 2$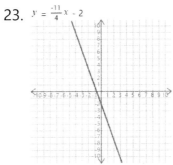

24. $x = -5$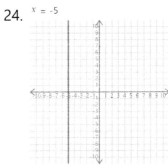

Slope-Intercept Form M1702-004

25. $y = \frac{-3}{4}x + 8$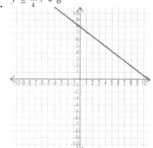

26. $y = \frac{5}{4}x - 4$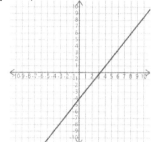

27. $y = \frac{3}{4}x + 5$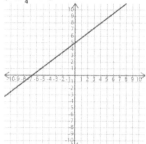

28. $y = \frac{3}{4}x - 5$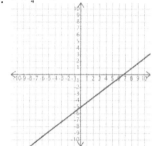

29. $y = \frac{-7}{4}x + 2$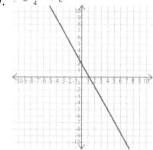

30. $y = \frac{5}{4}x - 8$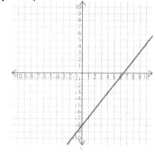

31. $y = 3x - 5$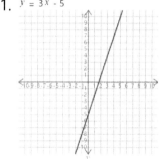

32. $y = \frac{-5}{4}x + 9$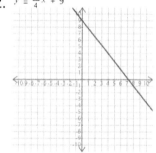

33. $y = \frac{-9}{4}x - 9$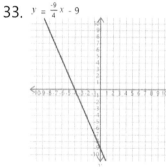

34. $y = -2x - 4$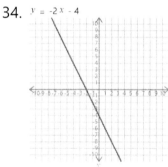

35. $y = \frac{-3}{4}x + 9$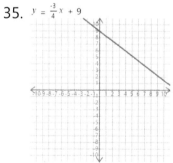

36. $x = -6$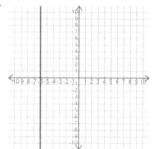

37. $y = \frac{-3}{2}x + 5$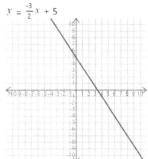

38. $y = -x + 9$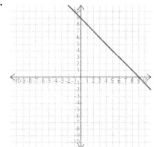

39. $x = 8$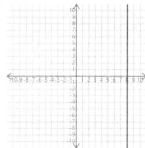

40. $y = \frac{1}{4}x - 10$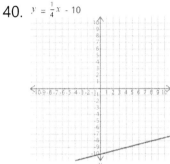

41. $y = \frac{7}{4}x - 4$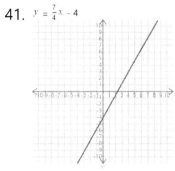

42. $y = \frac{-11}{4}x$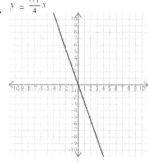

43. $y = \frac{5}{2}x + 2$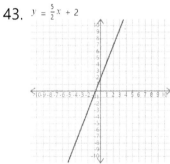

44. $y = \frac{9}{4}x - 3$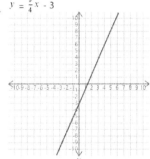

45. $y = \frac{-5}{4}x - 7$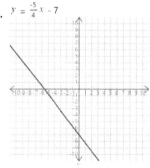

46. $y = \frac{5}{4}x + 10$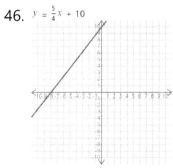

47. $y = \frac{-3}{2}x + 3$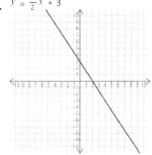

48. $y = -2x + 2$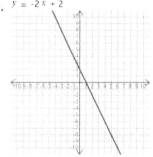

Slope-Intercept Form M1702-004

49. $y = \frac{1}{4}x + 4$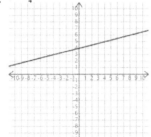

50. $y = \frac{-3}{4}x - 4$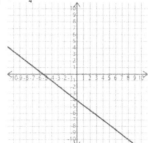

51. $y = \frac{3}{2}x - 2$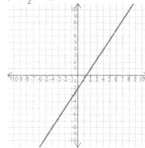

52. $y = -6$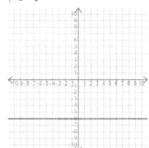

53. $y = 2x - 10$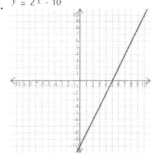

54. $y = \frac{-5}{4}x - 1$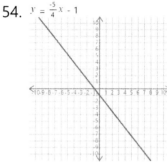

55. $y = \frac{-1}{2}x - 8$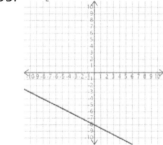

56. $y = -x + 8$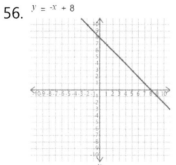

57. $y = \frac{-5}{4}x + 1$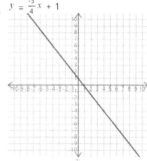

58. $y = 3x + 6$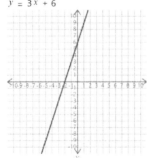

59. $y = \frac{-9}{4}x + 3$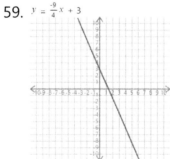

60. $y = \frac{-1}{4}x + 3$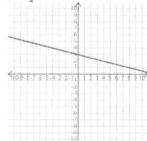

61. $y = \frac{11}{4}x - 9$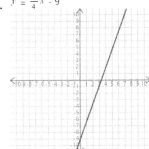
62. $y = \frac{-11}{4}x - 8$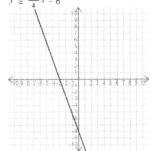
63. $y = \frac{-7}{4}x + 4$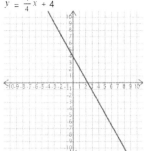

64. $y = \frac{7}{4}x - 2$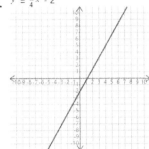
65. $y = \frac{-3}{4}x + 6$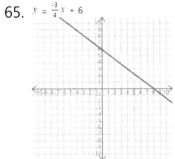
66. $y = \frac{5}{4}x - 2$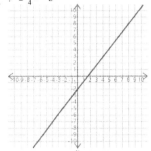

67. $y = \frac{3}{4}x + 3$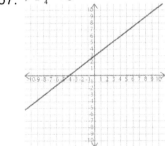
68. $y = \frac{-5}{2}x + 2$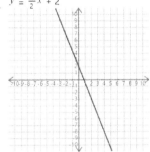
69. $y = \frac{1}{4}x + 6$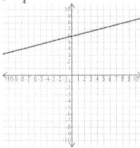

70. $y = \frac{-11}{4}x + 7$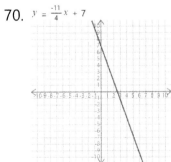
71. $y = \frac{7}{4}x + 1$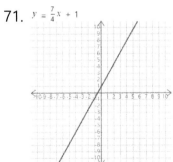
72. $y = x - 3$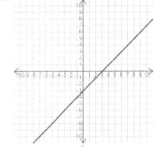

Slope-Intercept Form M1702-004

73. $y = \frac{-3}{4}x + 3$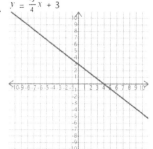

74. $y = x + 4$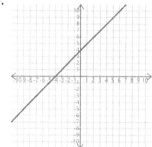

75. $y = \frac{5}{2}x - 8$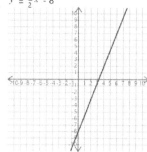

76. $y = +10$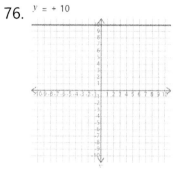

77. $y = -3x - 9$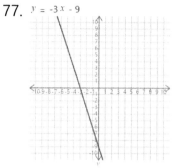

78. $y = \frac{-5}{4}x + 8$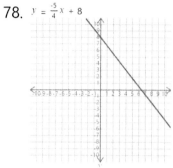

79. $y = \frac{-1}{4}x + 9$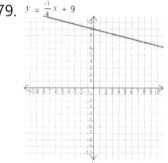

80. $y = \frac{-5}{4}x + 3$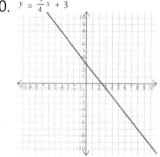

81. $y = \frac{5}{4}x + 1$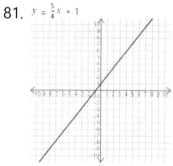

82. $y = \frac{-5}{2}x + 3$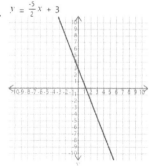

83. $y = \frac{1}{2}x - 9$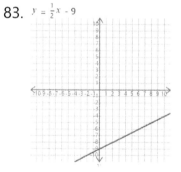

84. $y = -x + 1$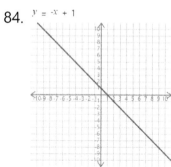

Slope-Intercept Form M1702-004

85. $y = \frac{1}{4}x + 7$
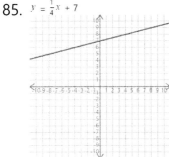

86. $y = -x - 8$
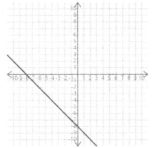

87. $y = \frac{7}{4}x + 3$
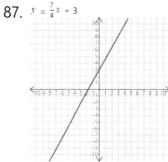

88. $y = \frac{-3}{2}x + 9$
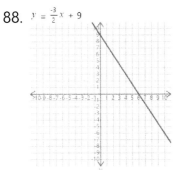

89. $y = \frac{1}{4}x$
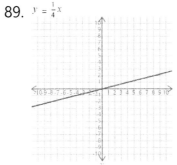

90. $y = \frac{3}{4}x - 1$
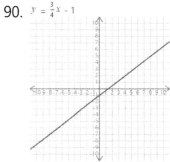

91. $y = 2x - 7$
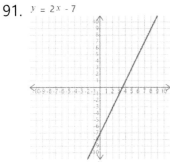

92. $y = \frac{-5}{2}x + 4$
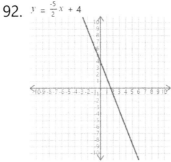

93. $y = \frac{-5}{2}x + 5$
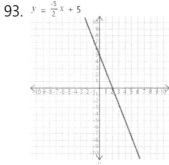

94. $y = -3x + 10$
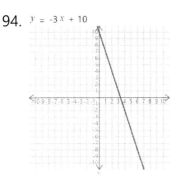

95. $y = \frac{1}{2}x - 1$
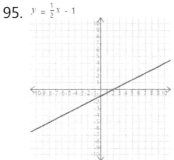

96. $y = \frac{5}{4}x + 8$
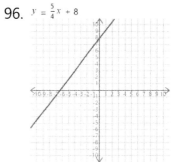

Slope-Intercept Form M1702-004

97. $y = \frac{9}{4}x - 7$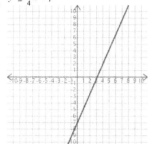

98. $y = \frac{-9}{4}x - 1$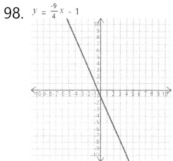

99.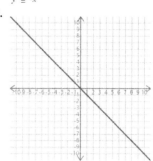

100. $y = \frac{-1}{2}x + 7$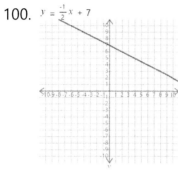

Printed in Great Britain
by Amazon

THE MAGIC OF LA BEFANA

ROSETTA SESTO
ILLUSTRATED BY ALENA KARABACH

© All rights reserved

"Nicola, come on!" said Emilia as she hung her stocking on the fireplace. Her little brother Nicola came down the stairs, rolling his eyes.
"I don't want to hang a stocking," he told her, "La Befana isn't real!"

"She is!" said Emilia, "Well, if you won't do it, I'll hang one for you. And for Lucia too." Baby Lucia who was snugly sitting on her dad's knee giggled loudly.
"Do you children want to hear the story about La Befana?" asked Dad.

"Yes!" said Emilia as she sat down in front of her dad on the rug.
"Alright, listen up," he said, "Do you remember the story of Baby Jesus? After he was born, three wise men came to visit him with many presents."
Emilia nodded. She remembered the story of the three wise men- the magi.

"Well, when the three wise men were traveling to Bethlehem, they stopped on the way to rest and have some food," said Dad, "An old woman named Beatrice Befana gave them shelter and food for the night. The magi were very grateful to her for helping them."
"Is Beatrice Befana La Befana?" Emilia wanted to know.

"Yes," Dad nodded, "The three wise men invited La Befana to come and visit Baby Jesus with them. But she could not join them because she had so much housework to do. So, she bid the men good luck on their journey and went on to continue with her housework."

"And then?" asked Emilia.
"Well, that night, La Befana was woken up by a brilliant light," Dad continued, "She took it as a sign to follow the three wise men to meet Baby Jesus. She packed some presents and flew off into the night on her broomstick."

"Did she find them?" Emilia asked.
"Sadly, no," said her dad, "She looked everywhere but could not find Baby Jesus or the magi. So, she gave the presents she brought to the other children who were sleeping. From then on, Beatrice Befana flies over the land on her broomstick on every Epiphany Eve."
"Does she come to Australia too?" asked Lucia, "I want to see her!"

"Of course, she comes here too," smiled Dad.
"She rides on her broomstick with one sack of lollies and one sack of coal," Emilia said, remembering what she knew about La Befana, "She gives lollies to the good children and coal to the naughty children. That's why we hang stockings- to receive her gifts!"

"Exactly!" smiled Dad, "On the night of January fifth, the Epiphany Eve, Beatrice Befana- or La Befana as we call her- comes to every home bringing lollies and coal. Some people say that she can make animals talk with her magic powers!"
"Meow!" said their cat Joshua, sounding surprised.

Their dog Tibby looked questioningly at Dad.
"Anyway," Dad said, standing up and putting Lucia down on the floor, "La Befana is going to be tired from her journey. So, we have to leave her some snacks and a glass of milk."

"I'm going to make some biscotti for her!" said Emilia as she stood up and ran to the kitchen.
That night, the family had dinner early. Emilia laid out the biscotti she made on a plate near the fireplace. She also placed a glass of milk there.

"Will La Befana come?" asked Baby Lucia.
"Yes, she will," Emilia said with a smile. Nicola rolled his eyes once again.
"Can I sleep with you today?" Lucia asked Emilia.
"Of course," said Emilia as she walked toward her room.

Sometime after she went to bed, Emilia woke up suddenly. She could hear the big clock downstairs striking midnight. She could feel something magical in the air. Turning her head, she saw that Lucia was awake too.

"I think something magical is happening!" said Emilia, "Maybe La Befana is here!"
"Let's go see!" cried Lucia, jumping out of the bed.
"Quietly!" said Emilia as she got out of bed. Together, they tiptoed out of the room and toward the stairs.

When they were halfway down the stairs, they could see the living room. A strange sound was coming from their chimney. Moments later, a brilliant glowing cloud came out from the chimney and landed outside the fireplace.

As Emilia and Lucia stared in surprise, the glowing cloud revealed an old woman, dressed in a white blouse, a long skirt, and a shawl. She was holding a broomstick in one hand and two sacks in the other hand.

"It's La Befana!" whispered Emilia.
La Befana slowly walked toward the plate of biscotti and helped herself to three of them. Then, she drank the whole glass of milk. After that, she went back to the fireplace where three stockings were hanging.

She opened her sacks and placed something inside each one of the stockings. The girls did not get to see what she put into the sacks because her back was turned to them. Just when La Befana was about to head back up the chimney, Tibby and Joshua came into the room.

"Hello there, nice doggy and cat," said La Befana, petting Tibby and Joshua, "Have you been good?"
"Yes, we have," said Tibby, wagging his tail. "I was a good cat too," said Joshua.

Emilia and Lucia were surprised to hear their pets speaking. But they remembered what their dad had told them about La Befana's magic making animals talk.
"I will be back next year to check on you two and the children," said La Befana.

Then, she went up the chimney, vanishing from sight.
Tibby and Joshua went on to talk about which one of them had heard La Befana coming down the chimney first.
"Can we talk with them too?" Lucia asked Emilia.

"I don't know..." said Emilia, thinking, "I think that might ruin the magic. Let's go back to sleep. In the morning, we can check what La Befana left us in the stockings!"
"Okay," nodded Lucia.
And so, they headed off to bed.

The next morning, they woke up later than usual. When they went downstairs, they saw Nicola stomping his feet on the floor.

"What's the matter?" asked Emilia.
"La Befana left him a lump of coal," Dad explained.

"That's because you were naughty!" Emilia told Nicola. She checked her stocking and was delighted to find lollies in there. Lucia's stocking also had lollies in it too.
"I can't wait to see La Befana next year too!" smiled Emilia as she put a lolly in her mouth.

THE END

Printed in Great Britain
by Amazon